PRAISE F
WHOLEHEARTED C

'This is such a lovely book. With beautiful heart-touching writing and many sweet and soothing illustrations (from Eliza Todd), Fleur Chambers has done it again, offering soulful guidance that is fresh, helpful, deeply grounded and wise, and comes straight from the heart.'

Rick Hanson, PhD, psychologist and author of *Resilient: How to Grow an Unshakable Core of Calm, Strength, and Happiness*

'Fleur has such a beautiful way of bringing together deep spiritual insights with practical day-to-day action - a rare gift! And her lived experience of finding confidence in her own voice is a true inspiration. This book will change you.'

Amy Taylor-Kabbaz, matrescence activist and author of *Mama Rising*

'A gentle paddle down the river of life with Fleur as your guide. Rest assured, you will be well looked after. Beautifully written and full of warmth and wisdom.'

Andy Hobson, meditation teacher and musician

'Fleur has a gift for taking tricky subjects like trauma, our shadow sides and self-worth and making them so relatable that the reader will feel empowered to make pivotal changes in their life.'

Jacqui Lewis, founder of The Broad Place and author of *The 14 Day Mind Cleanse*

'Hooray! Another beautiful heartfelt and healing book by Fleur Chambers. I encourage you to allow these wise words, glorious illustrations and suggested practices weave their magic in helping you create wholehearted confidence. The vulnerability, reflection and maturity shared in this book is precious.'

Dr Freya Bennett-Overstall, yoga and meditation teacher and author of *Wonder Full Women*

'In her soothing yet practical, wise and hilarious voice, Fleur Chambers introduces a new version of confidence that doesn't depend on other people's opinions and can't be diminished by perceived failure. *Wholehearted Confidence* sent me on a journey of discovering that right now, as I imperfectly am, I am not only enough but I am everything I should be. Get ready to step out of your limiting mind and into the expansive, magical world that Fleur invites us into.'

Christey West, co-founder of Just Peoples

'Fleur has an incredible talent for tricking you into transformation without making "the work" feel like work. This is the confidence cheat-sheet, a call to action to stop forcing and judging and, instead, soothe your way into a new kind of self-assurance.'

Amy Molloy, journalist, editor and author of *Wife, Interrupted*

'As I delved into the first few pages of *Wholehearted Confidence* I felt a unique excitement. Fleur's remarkable ability to infuse wisdom and warmth into her teachings makes her book a beacon of light on the path of personal growth. Her insights, drawn from her rich experience, offer a unique blend of practical advice and heartfelt encouragement.

I wholeheartedly believe that this book will be a source of strength, resilience and empowerment for anyone who reads it.'

Dr Vanessa Atienza-Hipolito, breast radiologist, clinical director and business owner of Women's and Breast Imaging and co-author of *Courage and Confidence*

'*Wholehearted Confidence* is deeply thought-provoking as Fleur takes you on a true journey of self-reflection and growth. The practices and illustrations encourage a subversive experience of self-love and perspective.'

Natashia Telfer, author of *Project Kind*

WHOLEHEARTED
Confidence

A NEW WAY TO LIVE, LOVE AND CONTRIBUTE

FLEUR CHAMBERS

THE FLEUR CHAMBERS COLLECTION

First published in Australia in 2023
By The Fleur Chambers Collection

A catalogue record for this work is available from the National Library of Australia

National Library of Australia Catalogue-in-Publication data:
Wholehearted Confidence/Fleur Chambers

Illustration and Cover Design by Elizabeth Todd
Book design by Bree Hankinson
Editing by Amy Molloy

978-0-6458670-5-3 (Hardback)
978-0-6458670-4-6 (Paperback)
978-0-6458670-6-0 (Ebook)

Disclaimer
The material in this publication is of the nature of general comment only, and does not represent professional advice. It is not intended to provide specific guidance for particular circumstances and it should not be relied on as the basis for any decision to take action or not take action on any matter which it covers. Readers should obtain professional advice where appropriate, before making any such decision. To the maximum extent permitted by law, the author and publisher disclaim all responsibility and liability to any person, arising directly or indirectly from any person taking or not taking action based on the information in this publication.

I dedicate this book to all my students,
who are, of course, also my teachers.

FOREWORD

Fleur gave me the gift of a new kind of friendship, one that I didn't know existed until she popped into my life.

I first met Fleur about six years ago, when I attended her Mindfulness for Mothers course in Melbourne, Australia. As a new mother I struggled with overwhelm, anxiety and imposter syndrome. My head was telling me all sorts of things that weren't helpful or reflective of reality. I now know that I wasn't alone in feeling this way. These limiting thoughts are so common for new mothers all around the world, causing huge suffering during one of the most profound times of life.

During this course, Fleur's teachings brought wisdom and perspective as well as practical tools to feel more peace and connection towards myself and my children. She delivered these gifts with hilarious frankness, and I just fell in love with her.

Our friendship has evolved beyond the teacher-student dynamic through invigorating walks on the beach and expansive paddle-boarding sessions, with each conversation bringing new insight into life's big questions or a humorous take on an old problem. I leave our encounters with a sense that I've just learnt an essential life lesson, but without heaviness and with a lot of fun along the way.

As well as our beautiful friendship, I also have the privilege of connecting Fleur with her philanthropic contributions through the charity I co-founded, Just Peoples. Fleur redistributes profits from her business to provide clean water to Bangladeshi communities whose basic needs are not yet met. Having provided more than 60,000 people with a permanent source of drinking water, Fleur wholeheartedly lives the values she teaches.

I've come to realise over time that Fleur is one of these people who intuitively encourages positive participation in the world at the same time as guiding me into a higher consciousness - where the things that usually stress me out simply don't matter. From this place, it's possible for me to access the profound love and joy that exist inside me.

I'm sure that as people read *Wholehearted Confidence* and make their way through the exercises, they'll feel Fleur's warmth and get to see life with newly opened eyes and hearts. Like me, readers will be guided to reconnect with what really matters to them and to their deeper, more peaceful self that cherises all the experiences that come with being human.

Johanna De Burca, co-founder of Just Peoples

CONTENTS

INTRODUCTION
1

REIMAGINE
19

BEFRIEND
65

GROW
133

EXPAND
185

EPILOGUE
265

Introduction

SHOULDERS BACK, HEART OPEN

Now is the time to embrace an understanding of confidence that normalises our human vulnerabilities, allows us to feel at ease amidst uncertainty and promotes a stronger sense of shared humanity.

I was part way through writing this book, at the stage when I would usually send it to my editor, when I realised ... I didn't need to. When I wrote my first book, I sent every draft chapter to my editor immediately. I was craving both guidance and validation. I needed someone to assure me I was on the right track, that what I had to say was worth reading. This time was different!

Whilst writing I felt quietly confident in my message, tone and position as an author. By the time you read this book, I will have sent my work to my editor - I do love and value her input - but without the desperate need for praise and approval, or for someone else to tell me that my perspective matters.

It was a milestone moment for me as I realised that I trusted my own voice and valued my expertise and experience. I also felt okay knowing that this book wouldn't appeal to everyone. It wasn't lost on me that I'd had this moment whilst writing a book on wholehearted confidence. To me, this is the version of confidence I've chased all my life - the type of quiet inner trust the world needs more than ever.

For many years, the prevailing advice for increasing self-confidence focused on the importance of voice tone, body language and self-belief. If you want to exude confidence, you need to speak with clarity and conviction. You must stand up straight. Make eye contact. Keep your chin up. Give a firm handshake. Command a wide-leg stance. Take larger steps. Sounds simple, right?

Perhaps you can even remember a time when you were feeling nervous before a meeting, presentation, difficult conversation, social event (or even a visit to the gym or local cafe) and a well-meaning colleague or friend suggested you 'put your shoulders back and hold your head up high', or you 'fake it till you make it'.

Whilst tempting in their quick-fix nature, we all know deep down that these 'tried-and-tested' steps don't really shift our inner confidence dial and can often feel forced rather than authentic. Why? Because none of this advice acknowledges the important role that the heart plays in feeling confident.

Take a moment to notice what happens to your heart when you take on these stereotypical postures of confidence. Try it now. Take a deep breath. Roll your shoulders back in a relaxed way. Allow a gentle smile to form across your lips. Notice how the space across your chest expands. Take another deep breath. Observe how from this position, there is more room for your heart - to feel, connect and lead.

Confidence is not about overly assertive body language and projecting ourselves and our opinions into the world. It's about having the courage to live, love and contribute wholeheartedly.

In a world characterised by climate crisis, racism and divisiveness, mental health challenges, and a collective experience of post-pandemic stress, fatigue, grief and loss, we need to move away from the clichéd and

SHOULDERS BACK
HEART OPEN

outdated notions of confidence. For example, that confidence includes commanding people's attention, exerting influence and always knowing the answer. Or that confident people, speak more than listen, prioritise individual achievement over collective good, don't experience self-doubt or imposter syndrome and never feel vulnerable.

Instead, it's time to cultivate the type of confidence that serves both individuals and communities - that encourages listening, flexibility, creativity and compassion. This book explores what I call *wholehearted confidence* - a more dynamic, gentle and necessary version of this inner quality. One that balances self-belief with compassion, self-assuredness with curiosity and individual achievement with being of service.

We need to embrace an understanding of confidence that normalises our human vulnerabilities, allows us to feel at ease amidst uncertainty and promotes a stronger sense of shared humanity. A version of confidence that includes our hearts and not just our egos.

Most of us have a long list of confidence prerequisites, stories that we have inherited, learnt or subconsciously picked up throughout our lives. Qualifiers like, *I'll feel confident when I ...*

- get that promotion at work.
- lose a few kilos.
- go to the gym more regularly.
- finish that online course.
- get rid of my inner critic.
- stop caring what people think of me.
- go back to work after having kids.
- receive praise from my boss.

- have a nicer home.
- find a partner.

Wholehearted confidence includes identifying our unique confidence qualifiers and seeing them for what they are - a collection of stories rather than truths. When we learn to break free from the conditions we have placed upon ourselves and our lives, we create space to experience a new, more real and meaningful version of confidence.

Let's try it together now. Take a deep breath and ask yourself, *What are my 'I'll be confident when ...' stories - the confidence prerequisites that are standing between me and a greater feeling of ease, acceptance and peace?* Give yourself a few minutes to reflect on this question.

How did that feel? Easy, hard, weird? Don't worry if that exercise felt challenging or strange. It's just the start. There will be lots of opportunities throughout this book to identify and let go of these outdated narratives, I promise.

I began to explore confidence - how we define it, who has it and what gets in the way - during a challenging period in my life that began about nine years ago. I spent much of my thirties and early forties struggling with chronic physical (and subsequent emotional) pain as I outlined in my first book, *Ten Pathways: A Framework for Redefining Happiness.*

Faced with a diagnosis with no cure, my world shrunk. The pain was so pervasive I was no longer able to work as a mindfulness and meditation teacher. I struggled to play with my young children. Domestic activities like cooking, cleaning, shopping and driving became increasingly difficult. Even catching up with friends felt hard as I was so distracted by the pain.

We've all got hills to climb

Unable to perform the roles that shaped my identity and afforded me a sense of confidence (like being a good mother, compassionate meditation teacher and loyal friend), my confidence began to erode. Emotional pain followed, as fear, anxiety and loneliness became my companions. I began to ask myself, *What type of mother am I if I can't play with, or cook for, my children? Who am I without my work? What type of friend am I if I'm totally distracted?*

As always, our challenges are rich learning opportunities. This difficult time in my life paved the way for fresh growth and new perspectives. Just like the lotus flower, three clear insights emerged from the murky waters of chronic pain.

1. Without those identities to wear like a comfortable cloak (mother, meditation teacher, friend), I began to get in touch with a deeper, wiser and more whole inner self, the me who didn't rely on external roles to feel self-assured, confident and enough.

2. Through the pain, loss, loneliness and uncertainty, there was a quiet strength, a gentle determination growing within me.

3. My challenges were making me more aware of the struggles of others. I began to connect with the idea of shared humanity. I felt more compassionate towards myself, others and the planet.

I began to wonder:

- What if our challenges and setbacks make us more, not less, confident?
- What if confidence isn't found by feeling in control, but by surrendering to the natural ups and downs of life?
- What if real confidence sounds more like a whisper than a roar?
- What if we used our sense of confidence to contribute to the world?

And finally, I asked myself:

If I let go of the old ideas and beliefs I have about confidence, will I feel more confident?

The answer was yes.

I began to explore these questions within my international meditation community through my meditation app, *The Happy Habit*. At first, I created one-off meditations to support people to develop a new, more real and enduring version of self-confidence. These meditations became so popular I developed an entire program dedicated to the pursuit of wholehearted confidence. It took a year to create as I wanted it to be so much more than a simplistic guide to banishing self-doubt and imposter syndrome. I was committed to helping people transform the way they felt about themselves, their lives and what it means to feel at home within your mind, body and heart.

This program soon became one of my most popular and impactful courses - and the inspiration for this book.

Over the years, I've been fortunate enough to support thousands of people around the world to explore their unique expression of confidence, how to embody it daily, and what gets in the way. When I decided to write this book, I reached out to my community, and people who had taken my course, to work more deeply with them, gather their feedback and track their experiences.

I am grateful for every student, and for every story and insight they shared, all of which helped me shape my four-part framework for wholehearted confidence.

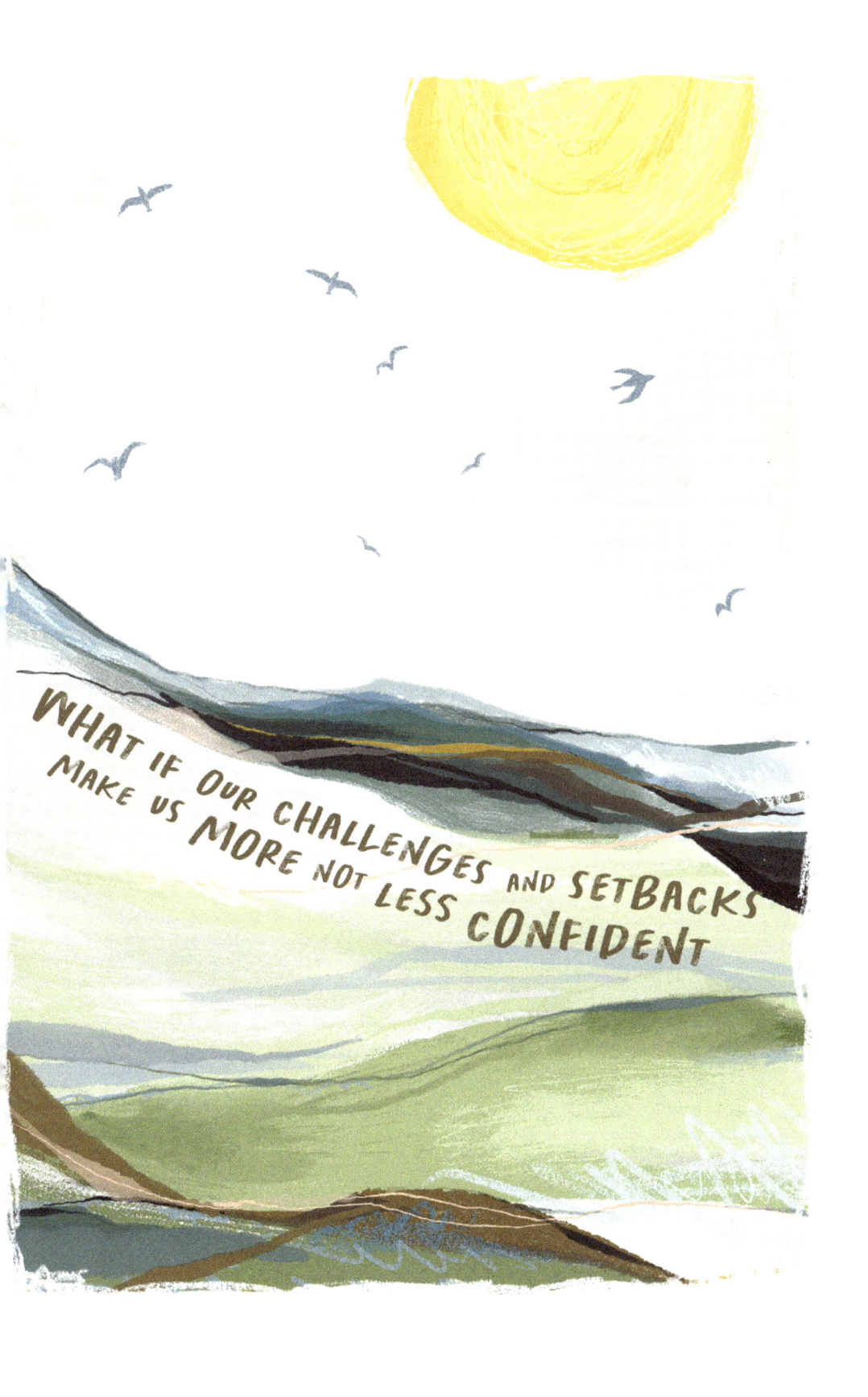

WHAT IF OUR CHALLENGES MAKE US MORE NOT LESS AND SETBACKS CONFIDENT

There are no composite or fictional characters in this book. Names have been changed for anonymity, but the details are all accurate. For me, these stories are the most important part of this book (so don't be tempted to skip over them!). It's one thing to learn the concepts behind wholehearted confidence. It's even more impactful to hear how people are living it in the real world - facing life's challenges, following their passions and improving their relationships thanks to a new confidence in themselves.

Part one is all about reimagining confidence and how you see yourself. You'll reflect upon your childhood and get curious about the positive and negative imprints these younger years have left on your adult self. You'll get clear on your values and practise weaving them into your everyday life.

Part two explores the liberating possibility that you don't need to eradicate your insecurities and vulnerabilities in order to feel confident. You'll learn how to identify these shadow aspects and attend to them with such curiosity and openness that they transform into wonderful teachers, guiding you to what is important.

In part three, you'll learn to balance out your inbuilt negativity bias and engage more skilfully with your ego. Together, we'll lean into our inherent goodness and our discerning nature so we can feel more confident within ourselves and our relationships.

Part four offers you the opportunity to break free from the constraints of your mind and open the lines of communication with your body, heart and the natural world. From here, you'll learn to hold your challenges and relationships in a much larger pool of awareness, leaving you feeling more confident, balanced and at ease.

This book contains lots of powerful mindfulness, visualisation and writing practices that have supported thousands of people just like you. They are designed to help you let go of the stories that no longer serve you, remember your deeper nature, expand into your full potential and feel more wholeheartedly confident.

If you usually avoid the practices in these types of books, I offer you a gentle invitation to give them a go. They will make all the difference and you will be surprised by what you learn about yourself. Don't forget, you oversee your own journey. So, if at any stage it feels too much, pause and take a break. There is no prize for getting to the end faster than what feels natural.

Wholehearted confidence includes listening to and trusting yourself. Make the practices your own. Get creative. And of course, you can do the exercises with a friend or therapist if you feel like the extra support would be of benefit to you. Finally, if this book makes you want to dive deeper, or you'd like to explore these ideas in meditation, you can access the complete course on *The Happy Habit* app.

Are you ready to develop the type of confidence that will allow you to feel at home in your body, mind and heart, whilst also making you a force of good in the world? Grab a notebook or journal. Set your expectations aside. Let's begin ...

BEGIN HERE
THE WHOLEHEARTED
POSTURE

So often we get caught in cycles of forward momentum, our attention like a laser, pointing at the next thing on our to-do list. When our mental and emotional focus is on the future, our physical posture changes. Often our head tilts forward, placing pressure on our neck and rounding our shoulders. From here, our gut can feel tight.

It's as if our physical body is mirroring our mental and emotional state. This idea that our thoughts, beliefs, attitudes and emotions can affect our physical body is referred to as the mind-body connection. We'll explore this connection throughout this book.

The wholehearted posture is designed to trigger a positive feedback loop between your body, mind, heart and environment. A key feature of the posture is a smile. Research suggests that a smile can spur a chemical reaction in the brain, releasing dopamine, endorphins and serotonin. These neurotransmitters are associated with lower anxiety and increased feelings of happiness. The smile we are learning to cultivate here isn't about 'faking it till you make it' or toxic positivity. It's more gentle and carries with it openness, ease and receptivity.

Begin by looking up at the sky. Take a deep breath. Sense into the expansiveness of the sky. Imagine that within the sky there is a smile. Maybe you can see a smile or feel the energy of friendliness, warmth or openness.

Now imagine that this smile is moving down from the sky and landing on your body. Soften your eyes. Allow the edges of your lips to turn upwards.

Take a deep breath and invite this smile to land across your shoulders, inviting your shoulder blades to drop down your back.

Notice how this naturally opens your chest (and your heart).

Repeat silently a few times: *Shoulders back, heart open.*

Allow the energy of the smile to soften your entire body.

Stay in this posture for a few breaths. Notice any experience of openness, ease or receptivity.

Now become aware of the earth beneath you. Offer your smile, your own sense of warmth and openness to the earth beneath you.

This wholehearted posture allows you to both receive and give a smile. It is a beautiful reminder of how connected we are to the sky above and the earth below.

LEARN TO
RECEIVE A SMILE
FROM THE
SKY ABOVE

Think of this posture as your travel companion as you journey through this book. We will start every practice in this way. You can also come back to this posture if at any stage you feel overwhelmed. It will relax your nervous system quickly. You might explore using this posture first thing in the morning or before bed at night. Notice what happens to your thoughts, emotions and wellbeing. Or weave it into your everyday, trying it when you are waiting for the kettle to boil, before a work meeting or a conversation with someone you love.

I've taught people all around the world this posture. Here's what they noticed:

- An experience of coming down from the mind into the body.
- An immediate softening of the ruminations and recriminations within the mind.
- A change in attitude, including feeling more optimistic.
- A willingness to circuit-break the internal drama.
- An ability to have hard conversations.
- A desire to speak more clearly and to articulate needs.
- A softening into the present moment, less need to hurry.
- A sense of pride for the body.
- Feeling straighter in the spine in a more visceral way.
- An experience of inner balance and harmony.
- Greater empathy for others.
- A willingness to let go of control.

You can also try this practice as an audio recording on *The Happy Habit* app. It might be a perfect introduction to meditation for you!

Part 1

REIMAGINE

Dare to see yourself as more than a collection of conditioned responses. It's time to return to wholeness.

If you've been interested in personal development for a while, the possibility that our childhood has an impact on how we see ourselves as an adult won't be new to you. Perhaps you've even seen these ideas diluted on social media or in everyday expression and now you feel skeptical, bored or numb when thinking about exploring your younger years as a way of understanding your adult self, your conditioned identity or your limiting beliefs.

Maybe your teenage kids tell you it's 'triggering' when you ask them to clean their room or do their homework. Perhaps you've heard people refer to a bad date or busy day at work as 'traumatic'. Have you read one too many quotes about loving your 'inner child'?

Or are you holding onto a common but faulty story - that only people who had a difficult childhood characterised by neglect, abuse, loss or disadvantage bring young scars into their adult lives?

If any of these perspectives ring true for you, I invite you to embrace your beginner's mind as we move through part one and two of this book. Referred to as *shoshin* in Zen Buddhism, the beginner's mind includes having an attitude of openness and a lack of expectation or preconceived ideas. In the context of this book, it's about seeing your childhood (and the imprints it left) with gentle eyes, a curious mind and a wise heart.

For moments from our childhood to leave a mark, they don't need to be dramatic - like divorce, the death of someone we love, a caregiver losing their job or moving schools. Often, it's the most mundane of comments or situations that can leave their imprint, especially during our formative years when we are developing our psyche. Like the time your mum told you to 'be more like your sister' or your father responded irritably to your tears with 'toughen up'.

These events, whilst seemingly small, can impact our sense of emotional safety, belonging and attachment. It's in these moments that many of us build our masks of self-protection.

Some common masks include:

- Putting the needs of others above your own.
- Pushing down emotions.
- Needing to get things right all the time.
- Procrastinating.
- Numbing out.
- Always being good.
- Using humour to appease stressful situations.

The truth is that we are all born into this world as fragile beings dependent on others for our survival. Much of our sense of self is formed through the interactions with those who provided primary care for us.

Given our parents or caregivers are human too, even if they had the best intentions to always attend to our needs, it's natural that there will have been times in our youth when our caregivers weren't perfect - times when we felt uncared for, unseen or unsafe. So, whether your younger years were characterised by love or loss, stability or change, consistent or unpredictable role models, we can all benefit from exploring our childhood as a way of understanding ourselves more deeply.

THE TRUTH IS THAT WE ARE
ALL BORN INTO THE WORLD
AS FRAGILE BEINGS
DEPENDENT ON OTHERS
FOR OUR SURVIVAL

TRAUMA IS NOT WHAT
HAPPENS TO PEOPLE

IT'S WHAT
HAPPENS INSIDE
PEOPLE

Before we begin to explore our childhood and the impact it's had on our experience of confidence as an adult, it's important to discuss trauma. The first thing to note is that trauma is not what happens to people (for example, living through war or experiencing family violence), it's what happens inside people because of these circumstances.

In his book, *Trauma and Memory*, Peter Levine, a leading trauma psychologist, confirms this internal focus when stating that trauma can:

> 'Alter a person's biological, psychological and social equilibrium to such a degree that the memory of one particular event comes to taint, and dominate, all other experiences, spoiling an appreciation of the present moment.'

Broadly speaking, there are two types of trauma - big T trauma and little t trauma. The former is the version that most people think of when they hear the word trauma. It occurs when things happen to vulnerable people (often children) that should not have happened. For example, abuse or neglect in the family of origin, racism, poverty, the loss of a parent or living through war or natural disasters.

In contrast, little t trauma relates to less dramatic experiences that have left a mark on people's inner landscape. For example, harsh comments by parents or being bullied at school. Interestingly, this version of trauma can occur through negative experiences or through a lack of good experiences, like feeling loved, safe or accepted.

REIMAGINE

It's worth noting that two people could experience the same event and one may feel stress in the short term, whilst the other may experience long-term trauma. This has less to do with resilience and more to do with our unique nervous systems.

As Dr Gabor Maté, trauma, illness and healing expert states in his book, *The Myth of Normal*, 'We each carry our wounds in our own way: there is neither sense nor value in gauging them against those of others.' Or, I would add, against our own expectations of what constitutes 'legitimate' cause for trauma.

An important aspect of walking the wholehearted confidence path is a willingness to step away from the story that trauma is an experience of 'other people' (not us). Instead, we need to walk towards the truth that trauma is common and that it exists as a continuum. Even with a predominantly happy childhood, many of us are on the trauma spectrum, even if we are miles away from the big T end.

Whilst this possibility may feel daunting for you, and you may be thinking, *Well now I feel even less confident*, the good news is that we can heal from trauma. That's because healing isn't about changing what happened to us in the past, it's about exploring our inner worlds: our emotions, somatic experience, coping mechanisms, internal scripts and conditioned identity. As Dr Maté explains, 'It's about returning to wholeness.'

Let's begin the process of connecting with our childhood together now.

Healing is A Return to WHOLENESS

MINDFUL PRACTICE
CONNECTING THE DOTS

Our subconscious mind stores thousands of memories. In meditation or in quiet reflective practices such as this one, it's possible to shine the light of awareness onto these previously hidden moments in time. When we are able to hold these memories in our non-judgemental awareness, whilst embodying the posture of wholehearted confidence, we can see these memories from our past, create space, unhook and perhaps even heal.

Settle into a comfortable position.

Begin by scanning your physical environment. Notice the roof over your head, the door, other aspects of your room that render you physically safe. Focus on elements of your room that afford you a level of comfort and ease. For example, books, pictures in frames, a rug or your pet. Take a few deep breaths into this feeling of safety, ease and belonging.

Close down your eyes. Embody the wholehearted posture (refer to page 14 if you need to). Imagine that the sky is smiling at you. Drop your shoulders down your back. Allow your chest and your heart to feel open and receptive. Send the feeling of a smile deep into the earth beneath you. Remind yourself that you are held by the sky above and the earth below.

Allow a memory from your childhood to emerge. Trust whatever appears. It may be a familiar memory or totally new.

Get curious. Reflect on the following questions:

- Was it night or day? Was I inside or outside?
- Was I alone or with others? What words were being spoken?
- What emotions were present for me and others? How did I feel in this moment as a child?

Take a few deep breaths. Connect with this younger version of you. Ask them: What do you need from me right now? How can I support you?

In your imagination, offer your younger self what they need. For example, a hug, reassurance, to be witnessed.

Open to any emotions or experience of comfort or healing.

Notice if this memory offers any clues or insights for you as an adult. How might this young experience have impacted how you see yourself and your life as an adult?

Reconnect with the wholehearted posture - the qualities of warmth and receptivity, your willingness to make connections and to understand yourself more deeply.

Repeat silently in your mind: *I acknowledge my childhood, whilst not being defined by it. I choose wholehearted confidence.*

You can explore this practice as many times as you like. Trust that your subconscious mind will reveal stories that you are ready to explore and learn from.

In my research, many people reflected upon how the words their parents (or siblings) used to describe them as children shaped their identity as teenagers and adults. Being told they were smart, shy or silly left a mark, impacting their thoughts, actions, relationships and sense of self.

'They're so smart.' Respondents shared how being constantly referred to as 'smart' whilst growing up impacted their experience of learning, achievement and success. When being smart was defined solely by getting perfect grades or topping the class, a love of learning disappeared, as did the ability to work collaboratively. As adults, people took this definition of smart with them into their work and their relationships. They got caught in black-and-white thinking. They competed rather than collaborated. Learning for learning's sake also felt unnatural.

'They're really shy.' For some, being told they were 'shy' by their parents contributed to a lack of self-confidence as an adult. People understood shyness and confidence as mutually exclusive ways of being. Taking this identity of shyness into their adult lives meant that people stepped away from challenges and new opportunities and didn't feel assured enough to take risks as a way of living with greater purpose and intention.

'Stop being silly.' Other respondents reflected upon the wound of being told they needed to stop being 'silly'. This message crept into adulthood, making it difficult for them to let go and have fun. Interestingly, this discomfort with fun also flowed into their own parenting as apprehension grew when their children became wound-up, playing and laughing.

'Be a good big sibling.' Sibling position also played a role in identity. Growing up in volatile family environments and being the eldest meant that respondents took on the role of protecting their younger siblings, often at the expense of their own needs. This energy of being hypervigilant about the needs of others was a theme that travelled into their adult lives.

'They're just a baby.' Interestingly, for others, being the youngest and treated like the 'baby' also left its mark. This learned experience of being taken care of by others led to feelings of shame when they needed help as an adult. In response, people swung to the other extreme, determined to be fiercely independent.

Finally, people recalled memories of when they expressed themselves through art, song, dance or sport and were criticised, put down or shamed. Rose, a member of my community, talked about her experience of being ridiculed when sharing her art and creativity.

CONFIDENCE IN ACTION - RECLAIMING YOUR CREATIVITY

Rose is seventy years old. She has loved painting since she was a girl. When she was young, she took delight in sharing her art with her family. She especially enjoyed painting scenes from the farm she lived on, depicting landscapes, people and animals with youthful exuberance.

In meditation, Rose recalled a day over sixty years ago. She was seven years old, joyfully sharing her latest painting with her family. Her brother (twenty years older than her) grabbed the painting, and in front of everyone, ridiculed her for how out of proportion the figures were, commenting that they 'ruined the entire painting'. Shortly after, Rose destroyed the painting because it was somehow 'tainted'.

From that moment, Rose stopped painting people or animals. Every time she tried, the brush poised over the paper, she just couldn't bring herself to do it. Anxiety and angst would wash over her in equal measure. For years, Rose told herself that the fear and discomfort came from being out of practise. But whilst exploring her past in the context of wholehearted confidence, she realised there was more to the story.

Rose connected with the unhealed wound of being shamed and ridiculed when expressing her creativity. She met the young part of herself who had been rejected. Rose commented, 'It's astounding how one small incident can make an everlasting impression on a child. How incredible that the source of that impression remains hidden, lost in time, yet the after-effect of the damage remains.'

Rose also reflected upon the impact that this feeling of not being safe to express herself had on her relationship with her brother. As an adult, she never felt totally comfortable in his company.

During the wholehearted process, Rose shared the regret she felt that her brother died before she could talk with him about this. She chose to forgive him 'for being an ass' and embraced the revelations that were emerging. Rose resolved to paint some animals and people in her work moving forward.

Interestingly, when chatting with illustrators for this book, many of them told me that they couldn't draw people or faces. I smiled and wondered where these stories came from.

I'm curious, is there a moment from your childhood when your joyful, creative energy was dampened? Was there a time when you became nervous about self-expression, confined by a belief that you aren't good enough? How could you start to reclaim your creativity?

BEYOND YOUR FAMILY

Growing up, it's not only our family or origin that impacts our identity. We are also influenced by friends, school, politics, television, magazines, and more recently, social media.

In my community, the most common experience people reflected upon was being bullied at school. Being teased and tormented for being overweight, too tall, too small or mixed race. Frightening moments behind the sheds or at the water fountain. Chipped teeth. Bruised knees. Harsh words straight to the young and impressionable heart. Decades later, the names and faces of these bullies still etched into the minds of both men and women.

When people in my community connected the dots, they discovered that these childhood experiences contributed to a number of adult challenges:

- Difficulty making friends later in life.
- A tendency to subjugate their own needs.
- Using humour to be accepted even when it felt unnatural.
- A lack of trust in female friendships.
- Body dysmorphia and eating disorders.

Ask yourself the questions below as a way to explore your own experience of social conditioning. You might want to think about the answers, write in your journal or notebook or even discuss them with your friends or partner - it can spark a fascinating conversation.

School

Were there moments in your school life when you felt left out, misunderstood or different? What coping strategies did you develop to survive these times? What feelings or beliefs have you taken from these experiences into your adult life?

Television/Movies

What television shows or movies did you watch growing up? Was there one or two that you really loved, perhaps playing on repeat? Looking back on these shows as an adult, what messages did you receive as a child?

Observing Grown-Ups

When you observed grown-ups in social or professional situations, what do you remember learning about class, social position or hierarchy? What did you learn (or assume) about what it took to be confident or successful?

THE WHOLEHEARTED CONTAINER

The purpose of reflecting upon your past is not to determine if you have experienced big T or little t trauma. Nor is it about blame, victimhood or objectively identifying cause and effect. Wholehearted confidence allows us to explore our past with curiosity, compassion, non-judgement and even forgiveness. It's an invitation to see the moments in our lives as stars amidst a beautiful constellation that is our life.

For me and thousands of others, exploring these ideas in meditation is a powerful way to drop into the moment, reflect and connect the dots. As one member of my community reflected:

> *'Recalling this period of my childhood within the safe, supported context of your guided meditation, my physical body grounded in the posture of wholehearted confidence, I was easily able to distance my true self from what happened to me. To see my past with new, more loving eyes.'*

Remember, the complete meditation course is available on *The Happy Habit* app, if, or when, you need it.

Interestingly, when people in my research group examined their past hurts whilst held in the energy of wholehearted confidence, many experienced a change in perspective and even forgiveness.

The schoolyard bullies were no longer powerful and loathing, instead, they were confused hurting children. Parents who weren't able to provide a stable home environment were no longer neglectful. They were people trying their best with the resources and opportunities they had. This certainly doesn't excuse traumatic or abusive behaviour, but forgiveness can put you on the path to healing and acceptance, rather than being caught in the disempowering cycles of resistance, blame and shame.

REIMAGINE

HAPPY MEMORIES & THE HEALING POWER OF CHILDHOOD JOY

So, how can we begin to soften the scars and heal the inner hang-ups? We can start by taking the time to think about what really brought us joy, hope and excitement as a child. We can reconnect with our youthful spirit and the aspects of ourselves that feel pure and whole. And as an adult, we can tap into these moments and memories to help us feel both happy and inspired.

In my community, people recalled all sorts of childhood delights.

- Riding bikes. Feeling the cool breeze. Being filled with a sense of freedom and excitement.
- Climbing trees as the sun went down.
- Walking in the forest for hours on their own.
- Rowing in a dinghy on a large, still lake.
- Hot summer nights on the beach.
- Badminton.
- Long walks with pets.
- Hiking and camping with friends.
- Dancing in the kitchen.
- Singing with family and friends.
- Taking calligraphy classes.
- Painting.

When you first try to think of what made you happy as a child, it might be hard to look past bruised knees and hurt feelings towards the moments when you felt a sense of vitality and belonging. Be patient and curious. Let's try it together now.

MINDFUL PRACTICE
STOKING YOUR INNER FLAME

This practice is an invitation for you to get in touch with your childhood delights – the hobbies, activities and rituals that allowed you to feel whole, safe and joyful. From here, you can get curious about how to weave these experiences and emotions into your adult life.

Take a few deep breaths. Settle into the wholehearted posture by imagining that the sky is smiling at you. Send this smile into your body and down into the earth beneath you. Imagine that the earth holds all the memories of your childhood delights.

Allow a happy memory to emerge from your childhood. This may be one that you visit often, a story you like to tell others about your past. Maybe it's a new memory that has taken you by surprise. Trust whatever has emerged.

Bring this memory to life by reflecting on these questions:
- Was it night or day? Was I inside or outside? Was I alone or with others?
- What exactly was I doing in this moment that allowed me to feel happy, joyful and present?

Picture a small flame in your heart. This small flickering light represents the young, happy, joyful aspects of you. Imagine that within your heart, this flame is getting bigger, brighter and more beautiful. Ask this flame: How can I bring more joy into my adult life?

Listen. Trust in what you hear, see or feel. Set yourself an intention for how you will bring more of your childlike essence, your spirit into your adult life as a way of embracing wholehearted confidence.

POSITIVE ROLE MODELS

Another way to explore positive childhood imprints is to reflect upon the role models we had whilst growing up. Cast your mind back to your childhood and notice if there were people who you admired or looked up to. Was there a teacher, family friend or celebrity who was good at sport, creative or musical? Was there someone who didn't care what other people thought of them? Perhaps you remember a particular person who had a positive outlook, even when they faced hard times.

Pick one person from your childhood who you looked up to and reflect upon these three questions:

1. What exactly did I admire about this person? (Skills, personality, outlook, the way they made me feel.)

2. What does this reveal to me about my own values, aspirations and deeper nature?

3. What lessons or ideas can I take from this into my adult life?

CONFIDENCE IN ACTION - CONNECTING WITH CHILDHOOD JOY

Anna grew up in Nigeria, Denmark and Australia. She spent much of her youth at a large Nigerian boarding school where she was the only student of mixed race. As Anna explored her childhood in meditation, many memories of being hurt, excluded and shamed for being different came to the surface.

Amidst the heavy memories, Anna also located many moments of joy as a child. Climbing trees, eating mangoes and guavas, jumping rope and playing badminton. These images came flooding back, warming her like the Nigerian sun. Rowing in the dingy, long walks in the heat with her dog, dancing to music in the kitchen, eating cereal whilst watching cartoons.

Anna also reminisced about the pure joy she experienced when having fruit fights. Clothes and skin drenched in the sweet, sticky fruit fibres. It was the Nigerian equivalent of a snowball fight. This memory, and the energy it held, was a gentle invitation for Anna to let go and have more fun as an adult.

During the wholehearted process, Anna also recalled how when she was young, she loved to knit baby boots with pompoms on them for babies. She collected leftover pieces of wool, taking delight in what she could create from what seemed like nothing.

She realised that within this memory was an invitation to knit again. To receive the warm hug that comes from wearing something you have knitted yourself. To experience the joy of giving something you have made to others. 'For me, knitting is almost like meditating. It brings me comfort. I create quiet and a space for epiphanies to creep in,' she explained.

Has Anna's story sparked a memory within you, reminding you of your own childhood delights? Were you happiest when out in nature, at home with your family or having fun with friends?

PEAK MOMENTS & YOUR CHANCE TO SHINE

So far, we've explored how childhood experiences can etch their way into our young psyches, over time building our conditioned identities and impacting our level of self-confidence.

Without judgement or blame, we've held these reflections in the container of wholehearted confidence, creating space for insight, healing and even forgiveness. We've also explored moments of childhood delight as a way of reconnecting with our deeper nature. The next step is to identify the moments in our lives that changed us, making us feel deeply alive, connected and aware of our values.

After knowing my now-husband for just one month, we set off on an adventure, travelling from Australia to Patagonia. Three planes, two trains and four boat trips later, we found ourselves in a remote part of Southern Chile, surrounded by soaring mountains, bright blue icebergs and golden grassland sprinkled with tiny yellow wildflowers and butterflies.

As we travelled through a mighty fjord in an army-grade inflatable, dressed in oversized waterproof pants held up by braces, I realised we had bypassed the romantic dating phase in our relationship!

The water was cold and perfectly still. The sheer cliffs on either side took my breath away. I remember a wave of awe and wonder washing over me, bringing with it a sense of peace and timelessness. The land felt prehistoric and sacred. I imagined seeing a neanderthal man wandering the side of the mountain in search of food. In that moment, linear time

THE BRIGHT STARS
SPARKLING AGAINST THE
ENDLESS DARKNESS
SPOKE TO THE DEPTHS
OF ME

dissolved. We stepped into 'soul time', the home of deep connection, intuition and oneness.

That night we camped beside the Grey Glacier, a thirty-two-kilometre stretch of the Southern Patagonian icefield. This glacier was more than eighteen thousand years old. Its colour resembled a precious stone. Our guide told us you could see the glacier from outer space – a sparkling blue mass.

I remember being tucked up in our tent, all warm and cozy in my sleeping bag, mesmerised by the soundscape. Hearing the iceberg groan, shift, crack and fall away into the lake, it was as if the Grey Glacier was alive. I imagined her breathing, expanding on the inhale, contracting on the exhale. I felt into the miracle that she had been doing this for thousands of years.

Energised by the life force radiating from the glacier, I got out of the tent and gazed up at the night sky. The bright stars sparkling against the endless darkness spoke to the depths of me. At that moment I felt small, insignificant and humble. I also felt part of the mystery.

Sixteen years later I look back on that day with gratitude, knowing it was what Abraham Maslow defined as a 'peak experience'. Moments that fill us with intense wellbeing, a feeling of wonder and awe, creativity and presence. He describes these moments beautifully when stating, 'The emotional reaction in the peak experience has a special flavour of wonder, of awe, of reverence, of humility and surrender.'

In her research, psychologist Gayle Privette identified three characteristics of peak experiences – fulfilment, significance and spirituality. She discovered that peak experiences generate positive emotion, they allow you to feel at one with the world, connected and more self-aware.

In these moments we wake from the trance of busyness and realise just how precious life is. Our daily complaints and ruminations about the heavy traffic, our demanding boss or our aging body feel small and insignificant. Peak experiences are like a lightning bolt of perspective, illuminating our desire to live a bigger, bolder and more aligned life.

But we all know that often these peak moments, and the internal shift they create, don't last. We return from an awe-inspired holiday and before long we are complaining about our endless inbox and the dirty washing. We bring our newborn baby home from the hospital and the feelings of unbridled love and connection get buried by fatigue and overwhelm. Wholehearted confidence includes keeping these feelings alive, taking the wisdom and replicating it amidst our ordinary everyday life.

That night in Southern Patagonia sixteen years ago, I connected with the mystery contained in the night sky and the life force radiating from the Grey Glacier. My perspective expanded as I began to understand that everything in nature contains the same universal energy.

I realised that when we connect with this sense of aliveness, our troubles feel smaller, we experience more peace and our sense of possibility magnifies. I've used these gifts many times throughout my life, in times of challenge, in ordinary everyday moments and in my meditation practice.

Learn to take
the wisdom from
your peak
experiences
into your
ordinary
everyday
life

In the weeks after I had COVID-19, I often found myself awake at night, my heart pounding and my mind racing, wondering if I was ever going to fully recover. Desperate for some reprieve, I would go outside and shift my gaze upwards to the night sky. Immediately the anxiety would soften and my perspective would expand. My tiny racing heart felt so small yet also held by the universal energy of love and compassion.

I also weave the night sky into my early morning trip to the bakery for the kids' school lunches. Each morning I pause, look up and smile at how life can be domestic and filled with routine, whilst also blessed with mystery.

And finally, the experience of moving from linear time to soul time whilst cruising through the fjord in Southern Patagonia has been a memory I have taken with me and weaved into my meditation practice.

Perhaps as you've been reading this your own peak experience has come to mind? Maybe you've reflected upon the birth of a child or grandchild, or a wilderness adventure that left you feeling awestruck and deeply aware of what really matters to you? Writing helps us to understand the significance of these experiences. Let's find our peak together in the next practice.

WRITING PRACTICE
FINDING YOUR PEAK

Set aside ten to fifteen minutes. Trust that this time will be well spent and that at the end, you will feel inspired! Take a moment in the wholehearted posture. Sky. Body. Earth.

Think back to a time when you felt alive, present and receptive. Perhaps it was a time you experienced a rush of love, peace, excitement or connection? Maybe you were with family, friends or in nature?

Now put pen to paper and answer the following questions:

• What gifts did this moment give me?

• What did this moment reveal to me about how I want to live and what's important?

• How can I bring the learnings and good vibes from this peak experience into my everyday life?

Finish by making a commitment about one way to bring this peak experience into your life. For example: *When I walk the dog after work, I will take the time to notice the sky and remind myself that life is expansive and full of possibilities.*

You might like to put this commitment on a Post-it Note or as a screensaver on your phone – keep your peak experiences alive and notice yourself feel more wholeheartedly confident!

IDENTIFYING & LIVING YOUR VALUES

As you've been reflecting on your childhood and your defining moments, you might be getting a sense of your values – the fundamental beliefs and intentions that govern how you live, love and work – kindness, creativity, humility, autonomy and so on.

When life is full and we are focused on our to-do list and what feel like endless responsibilities, our values can get buried beneath the busyness. An important aspect of wholehearted confidence is taking the time to get clear on your values and using these as an inner compass.

We can use our values to:

- support us in times of challenge or uncertainty.

- guide decision-making (mundane and significant).

- improve our relationships.

- steer us towards activities and experiences we really enjoy.

- encourage us to work towards bigger goals and aspirations.

Given our values change as we do, it's worth spending a few minutes identifying and spotlighting them. You might be surprised by what emerges!

WRITING PRACTICE
YOUR VALUES CHECK-IN

Allow the energy of a smile to wash over you, moving from the sky above into the earth beneath you.

Cast your eye across the list to your right. Breathe deeply. Allow seven values from the list to grab your attention. Try not to overthink this, trust whichever values emerge from the list. Write these down. Look over your list. Now reduce the list to just four key values. Write these down.

With these four values in mind, reflect on these points:

1. For each of the four values, write a statement about how you could bring this value to life each day. For example: *I will bring a sense of **joy** into the way I parent, creating space for more fun and ease with my children.*

2. Think about a current challenge or a general point of tension in your life. Write about how you could use these four values to help you navigate this situation. For example: *When reflecting on my strained relationship with my mother, I can use the value of **freedom** to let go of past hurts, disappointments and resentments.*

3. Think about something you aspire to. Write about how any of these values could help you experience these aspects of life you desire. For example: *When I am tempted to put off my meditation or yoga practice, I remind myself that **spirituality** is one of my values.*

It's important to remember that there is no hierarchy when it comes to values. As we go through the seasons of life, it's normal for our values to shift. A problem only arises when we don't acknowledge the change and cling to values that no longer align with our life stage.

LOYALTY

ADVENTURE

FORGIVENESS

FLEXIBILITY

SOLITUDE

GRACE

TIME

FREEDOM

HOPE

MEANING

EMPATHY

AUTONOMY

CALMNESS

CURIOSITY

ACCEPTANCE

OPTIMISM

KNOWLEDGE

AWE AND WONDER

PEACE

PLEASURE

COMMUNITY

FREEDOM

VITALITY

JOY

GRATITUDE

TRUTH

CREATIVITY

RESILIENCE

PURPOSE

COMPASSION

LEADERSHIP

LOVE

ACHIEVEMENT

HUMOUR

TRUST

PLAY

BALANCE

PERSISTENCE

GENEROSITY

WISDOM

HUMILITY

SPIRITUALITY

EXCELLENCE

MINDFULNESS

SELF-REGULATION

KINDNESS

CONTRIBUTION

INTEGRITY

HONESTY

HEALTH

LEARNING

APPRECIATION

FUN

HUMANITARIANISM

CONNECTION

SELF-CARE

COURAGE

PATIENCE

PERSPECTIVE

COLLABORATION

INNER HARMONY

FROM COMPARISON TO
SHARED HUMANITY

So far, we have explored wholehearted confidence by looking inwards, to our past, our values and our deeper nature. The truth is the human mind loves to turn its gaze outwards and compare. In Buddhist psychology this practice is called *conceit* and is believed to cause harm. By comparing our lives to those of our friends, colleagues, relatives or even strangers, we abandon the safety and peace that is found in our wholeness.

The mental infliction of comparison is exhausting in its never-ending nature. It often begins in childhood when our parents make comments like, 'Why can't you be more like your sister?' or, 'You are the clever one, your brother is the sporty one.' By the time we reach adulthood the comparisons come from all directions. As one respondent commented, 'It was a double-edged sword that I turned on myself.'

Whilst eating breakfast, we scroll through social media and see a manufactured glimpse of someone else's life. It can feel as though everyone is having peak experiences all the time! Even though we know these images aren't real, we still feel like our lives are routine driven or lacking adventure in comparison.

It's not only 'upward comparison' we fall into (when we compare and feel inferior to another person). It can be equally detrimental to 'downward compare' and think of ourselves as superior to someone who we perceive as lacking. Mainstream wellbeing publications tell us a 'downward comparison' is better for our self-esteem ... but is it really? Check in with your body the next time you do it. Or even better, check in with your heart.

We drive to work and see a parent telling their kids to 'hurry up and get in the car', and we think to ourselves, *I got the kids off to school today without any drama.* At work, we hear a quiver in a young colleague's voice when they speak in meetings. We smile and think to ourselves, *I never get nervous speaking in public.*

Take a moment now to consider how long that injection of subtle superiority actually lasts. I'm curious, does it create an enduring experience of self-esteem? I doubt it. Because that short burst of 'confidence' you receive comes from judging someone else harshly. And if you're honest, you're probably more alike than you are different.

In her book, *Loving Kindness*, Sharon Salzberg, a leading spiritual teacher, reflects on the painful restlessness that emerges from comparisons. She states:

> *'Whether we conclude that we are better than, worse than, or equal to another, when we measure ourselves against others, there is no peace. Any act of establishing our status in reference to others creates stress as at any moment someone else could enter the picture!'*

So, how can you begin to soften this unhealthy (and exhausting) habit? The first step involves getting to know your unique habits of comparison. As with so many mental habits, they play on autopilot without us even noticing. So, taking time to bring them into the light of awareness is an important first step. You can do this by reflecting upon the three questions below. As always, you can write your responses down in your journal, or just think about them for a moment now.

1. In what aspects of my life do I get most pulled into the energy of comparison? For example, at work, socially, at family gatherings or when on social media?
2. Do I more often make upward or downward comparisons?
3. How do these comparisons make me feel about myself and my life?

The second step is to intentionally unhook from these internal narratives, and instead, open to the idea of 'shared humanity' - an acknowledgement that we all carry the same deep desire to be seen, heard and recognised for who we are. The belief that we all deserve to experience freedom, hope, dignity and purpose in our lives. The truth that we will all experience both joy and sorrow.

So, next time you notice yourself comparing, pause, take a breath and shift your thinking. Begin by saying something to yourself like: *I let go of these comparisons because they are not helpful.* Then look for ways that you and this person are more similar than different. For example, perhaps you both want to feel loved, respected or seen for who you are? Maybe you have both been through a hard time or had something to celebrate recently? Spend a few moments focusing on these things, rather than on your differences.

Breaking habits of a lifetime takes patience and repetition. Think of training a puppy to sit before crossing the road. You have to gently tell it to sit many times before it knows how to do it on its own. It's the same with comparisons. We need to train our brain. So how will you know if it's working?

Broadly speaking, it will feel like moving from contraction to expansion, or a feeling of tightness to a feeling of being more open. More specifically, you might notice:

- your body relax as you circuit-break the comparing thoughts.

- a feeling of relief.

- the voice of inner judgement becomes quiet for a moment.

- a lightness in your heart as you let go of the burden of feeling unworthy or not enough.

- the humour in it all, how ridiculous some of the comparisons we make are.

- how much your mind really is like a puppy!

If the idea of shared humanity and connecting with qualities that transcend our upbringing, culture and personality feel abstract, esoteric or out of reach, that's okay. In my experience and with people I've worked with all around the world, it's useful to begin from a more biological standpoint.

Take a moment to consider that there are over seven billion people on the planet and that every one of us, no matter our nationality, ethnicity, gender or life experience, is 99.9% identical in terms of genetic make-up.

Every one of us breathes all day every day. Our hearts beat. Many of our emotions are universal, and the way our faces express core emotions are hardwired into our genes.

Research also highlights the neurological evidence that, as humans, our brains are designed to cultivate connection with others. In his book, *Social: Why Our Brains Are Wired to Connect*, psychologist Matthew Lieberman explores the neural networks devoted to different aspects of social connection. He posits a basic working definition of shared humanity - no matter who we are or where we are from, we all feel, think and can empathise with others.

So, whether you feel drawn to connecting to our shared genetic make-up, neurological structures for connection or deep desires to feel seen or heard, I hope you'll explore what it feels like to shift from the energy of comparison to shared humanity.

Remember, as humans, we will all have moments of joy, sadness, excitement, hope, dread and sorrow - we all want to feel loved, appreciated and recognised for who we are. Lean into these ideas next time you notice yourself hooked into upward or downward comparison and when you do, offer yourself a smile for embracing wholehearted confidence. Let's practise unhooking together now.

VISUALISATION PRACTICE
TWO HEARTS TOGETHER

Settle into the wholehearted posture. Take five breaths here. Think of someone you often compare yourself to (either upward or downward). Picture the clothes they wear, the things they say and do. Recall all the stories you create in relation to this person.

Take a few more deep breaths. Imagine that this person is sitting next to you. Remind yourself that genetically, you are almost identical. Picture both your hearts, beating at the same time.

Look up at the sky above you both. Imagine that all the comparisons you make about this person are like clouds moving across the sky. As the clouds pass, the stories of comparison soften.

You can see that the sky is smiling at you both. This sense of warmth and possibility shines down on the two of you. Acknowledge that within both of your hearts is a deep desire to be seen, heard and recognised.

Repeat silently in your mind: *I let go of all the stories, and instead, I acknowledge you.*

Remind yourself that this person, simply by being human, will experience both joy and sorrow in their lives. They will go through periods of self-doubt, insecurity, disappointment and regret. They will also experience times of happiness and success.

Repeat silently: *May you face your challenges with a open heart. May you enjoy the good times. I wish you well.*

Notice any feeling of expansion within your body, mind or heart.

Trust that doing this practice regularly will encourage a shift within you. As one participant reflected,

> 'I always thought my problems and issues were unique character deficiencies that others did not have. Doing this practice offered me a visceral experience, allowing me to connect with the possibility that we are more the same than different.'

PART ONE: SELF-REFLECTION

As part one draws to a close, take a few moments to think about the fundamentals of what we've learnt so far. After completing this part of my online course, here are some of the ways people within my community described wholehearted confidence:

- Learning to give myself the attention, time and love that I so freely give to others.
- Accepting that I am a work in progress and that I can feel confident, even when I don't have all the answers.
- Seeing vulnerability and not knowing as an open field of possibility rather than a limitation.
- Setting boundaries around work so that I can be present for my family and friends and live out my core values each day.

Take a few minutes to reflect upon these four questions. Write your response down in your notebook or journal.

1. What is my definition of wholehearted confidence?
2. What are my core values?
3. How can I replicate the joy of my childhood in my everyday life?
4. How can I bring myself back from a place of comparison?

YOUR
CONFIDENCE
COMMITMENTS

Repeat the below phrases to yourself, either out loud or in your mind, in the morning or at night. Write them in your journal or on a Post-it Note. Use them anytime you want to drop into the feeling of wholehearted confidence.

I acknowledge my childhood, whilst not being defined by it.

I remember the happy moments from my childhood and commit myself to bringing these feelings into my adult life.

I am willing to explore my conditioned identity and soften the protective habits that no longer serve me.

I use my values to guide my actions.

I move from comparison to shared humanity each day.

Part 2
BEFRIEND

Dance with your shadows until they transform into something beautiful.

Everywhere we turn our gaze, we are receiving messages (both subtle and strong), that to feel confident, we need to eradicate all self-doubt, imposter syndrome or fear of being judged. We start to believe we must get rid of all these 'shadows' and become a constantly bright beacon of positivity and self-belief to be successful, and therefore, confident.

Of course, this isn't possible, and before long, we go to war with that voice in our head telling us we aren't good enough. We are hard on ourselves when we feel nervous before an important work meeting. We tell ourselves that if we were truly confident, we wouldn't care what other people thought of us. We would step into a new career, creative project or relationship with assuredness and ease.

Wholehearted confidence offers a different (and refreshing) way to interact with our insecurities. Rather than seeing their presence as a sign of our own failure or as a roadblock on the path to feeling comfortable in our own skin, this version of confidence includes accepting these aspects of ourselves and ultimately, learning from them.

Wholehearted confidence is a brave invitation to hold our humanness with such curiosity that ultimately, our shadows become our wise (and often humorous) teachers. I find this idea – that *real confidence* is about being with it all, the light and the dark, the assuredness and the insecurities – a huge relief.

WHOLEHEARTED
CONFIDENCE
ALLOWS US TO
BEFRIEND OUR SHADOWS
WITH SUCH CURIOSITY
THAT OVER TIME,
THEY TRANSFORM INTO
OUR WISE
TEACHERS.

It's a giant yes to every aspect of ourselves and our entire human experience. Interestingly, the majority of people in my meditation community felt this sense of relief too.

So, after a lifetime of disliking that little voice inside our heads, after years of telling ourselves that successful and confident people never feel like an imposter or a fraud, how do we begin to develop more wise relationships with these shadow aspects of ourselves? How do we make room for them so that we can access their wisdom?

Part two of this book teaches you the exact four-step framework I developed - dancing with your shadows. It also provides you with some raw and honest examples of how people all around the world have used the framework to navigate and learn from their insecurities and vulnerabilities. Perhaps you'll smile as you see aspects of yourself in their stories.

DANCING WITH YOUR SHADOWS - A FOUR-STEP FRAMEWORK TO NAVIGATE YOUR HUMANNESS

This is a spiritually informed, mindfulness and somatic-based framework I developed for identifying, exploring and learning from your humanness.

I've been told by some community members that it compliments Internal Family Systems – a transformative tool developed by Dr Richard Schwartz that helps people understand their protector and wounded parts. Other students have shared how exploring this framework has deepened their spiritual practice and capacity for self-acceptance and compassion. And those students without an interest in psychotherapy or spirituality have found the experience illuminating, rewarding and deeply satisfying.

The four steps for dancing with your shadows are:

1. Identify and welcome.

2. Meet it in your body.

3. Be honest.

4. Access a deeper truth.

I know it can be tempting to skip to step three or four, because you think you already know your shadow and how it feels in your body, but I do encourage you to go through all the steps. The insights will be richer and more complete.

If you would also like to be talked through the process, you can explore this framework in the *Wholehearted Confidence* course on *The Happy Habit* app.

As with part one, if you are feeling nervous about meeting your shadows, you can try this practice with a friend or therapist. Remember, you can take it at your own pace and if the experience feels too strong, return to the wholehearted posture for a few breaths and allow the smile from the sky to bring you back to a sense of safety.

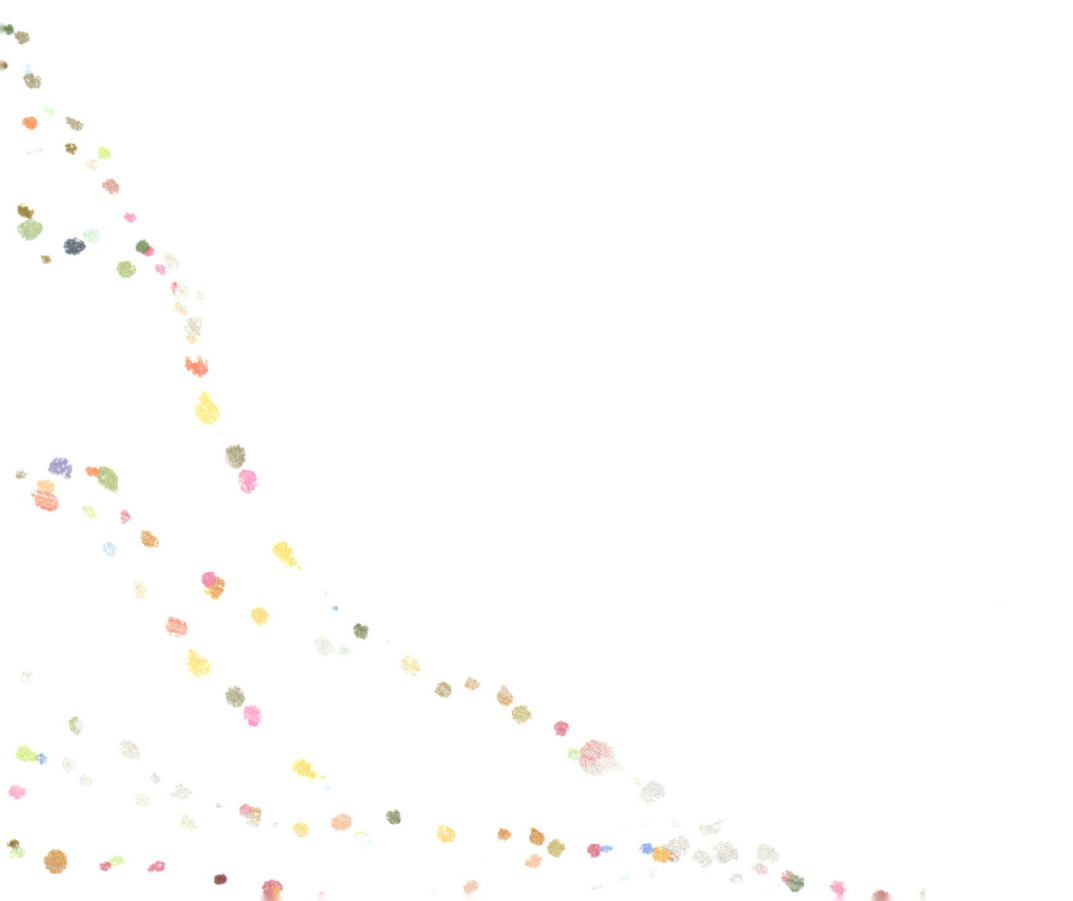

STEP ONE - IDENTIFY & WELCOME

The first step is to identify your shadows, these parts of yourself that you don't particularly like or accept, inner aspects that you often hide from others, feel embarrassed about or ashamed of. Whilst many of these shadows are interrelated, in my research I was able to place the most common shadows under three key headings:

Not enoughness.

Imposter syndrome.

High expectations.

Now you might be thinking that identifying your shadows seems like an easy task. But in truth, these aspects of ourselves have often been around so long that we actually see them as part of our personality.

For example, if you say things like, 'Oh, I'm always hard on myself, it's just who I am,' you may be surprised to discover that this isn't your core personality - you are just over-identifying with the not enough shadow.

If you identify as someone who needs to get things perfect to feel satisfied, exploring the shadow of high expectations might allow you to see yourself in new and liberating ways.

Identifying our shadows requires a sense of openness and curiosity, a willingness to see the aspects of ourselves that we have long hidden or resisted with kinder, more accepting eyes. Let's start gently together with the following practice.

WRITING PRACTICE
GETTING TO KNOW
YOUR SHADOWS

Set aside ten to fifteen minutes. Make yourself a cup of tea, turn on some music, whatever you need to get in the mood. Respond to these questions in your notebook or journal. If you feel like exploring all three shadows at once is overwhelming, you can choose one of the headings below, which resonates for you, and focus on those questions. Come back to the others another time.

NOT ENOUGHNESS

- Do you find it difficult to accept yourself just as you are? Write about a time when you felt like you weren't enough.
- Do you try and be more than what feels easy and natural (more productive, organised, disciplined, intelligent, skilled, reliable, kind, funny)? Describe how this plays out in your life.
- Do you have a 'not enough' narrative that is playing in the background most days (not slim enough, smart enough, successful enough, interesting enough)? Write this narrative down and explain when you feel it the most.
- Do you sometimes see life through the lens of scarcity? For example, when someone shares their success, is there a part of you that is worried there won't be room for you to be successful too? Describe a time recently when you felt this way.

IMPOSTER SYNDROME

- Do you downplay your achievements or attribute your success to luck or timing? Describe a time recently when you did this.
- Do you worry that you are going to be found out, that people will discover that you are not the real deal? If so, write about when this feeling is strongest.
- Do you have trouble receiving external praise? Make a note of the last time you rejected a compliment or pushed back on kind words.

HIGH EXPECTATIONS

- Do you often get to the end of the day and feel disappointed in yourself, in how you acted, what you did or how much you achieved? Write about how this makes you feel.
- Do you replay conversations and wish you had acted differently? Explore how this affects your sense of self.
- Do you over prepare or overplan your week as a way of feeling in control? Is this an old or a new habit? Write about where it might come from.

NAMING YOUR SHADOW

To my surprise, when I asked people in my community to name their shadows, their responses were creative and humorous. For example:

Anna Anxiety.

Chrissie Babble.

Kurt.

False Cassandra.

Ms Guardian.

Doubting Deb.

Blaming Bertha.

Charlie My Wild Side.

Scaredy Cat.

Paper Tiger

Grumpy Control Freak.

Morning Dread.

Devil on One Shoulder.

These responses made me smile for two reasons. Firstly, they revealed people's capacity to tackle a potentially heavy topic with lightness. Secondly, they showed a willingness to create space between themselves and their shadows. With space comes choice and ultimately freedom to break free from the over-identification with these aspects of ourselves.

Now it's your turn. Pick the shadow that is speaking to you most strongly and give it a name. (There are no silly answers!)

STEP TWO - MEET IT IN YOUR BODY

The second step is to explore how this shadow feels and expresses itself in your body. It's best to do this in real time as you experience the shadow. But for now, let's use our memory and imagination. Think back to a time when a shadow swept over you (a time when you felt like you weren't enough or that you would be caught out) and reflect on these questions:

- Where do I feel it in my body?

- Does it have a colour, shape or texture?

- Is it moving or still?

- What words would I use to describe it? Rough, smooth, sharp, dull, blunt, opaque, see-through, shiny, heavy, light and so on.

There is no right or wrong way to explore felt sensations or to connect with the imagery that may arise. Trust your own ability to locate this shadow in your body. Remember, if the sensation feels too strong, you can always move your attention to a part of your body that feels more neutral or to the image of the sky above smiling at you. Exploring your shadows as part of wholehearted confidence includes trusting that you know when to move in and out of this four-part process.

When I asked my community how they experienced their shadows physically, it varied - a lot! As you can see from the following lists, shadows can find home in different parts of our bodies and present in a diverse range of ways.

PHYSICAL MANIFESTATIONS OF THE SHADOWS:

- Heavy weight in the upper body.
- Pressure across the eyes.
- Nausea in the gut.
- It begins in the mind, then it wraps itself around the body.
- A weight across the shoulders.
- A sinking feeling deep in the stomach.
- A lump in the throat.
- A hot, red feeling on the face.
- Numbness.
- Pain across the upper back.
- Soreness in the hips.

Disclaimer: some of these symptoms can also be linked to serious medical conditions, so listen to your body and take responsibility for seeking guidance from a medical professional.

VISUAL REPRESENTATIONS OF THE SHADOWS:

- A heavy cloak.
- A big ugly smudge.
- Dark, heavy rainclouds.
- Thick, braided beige rope with sharp strands of jute pointing outward like wiry thorns.
- A greenish presence with surgically sharp edges.
- A dark brown mud.
- A heavy, burgundy coloured curtain of fear.
- A ball of yarn.
- A set of nested Russian dolls.
- Mirages of danger in my mental map of the universe.

- 'It's a chameleon - anything bright and shiny to lure me away from what I want to accomplish.'
- 'Charlie is like the wind, always moving, changing speeds and impacting the environment.'
- 'It's like a vacuum sucking up all and any motivation to understand, improve or feel creative.'
- 'It is a jitteriness – like discordant notes being played on a piano.'
- 'It feels like a vortex or tornado, spinning around.'
- 'It covers me like a skin, immobilising me into inaction.'
- 'This shadow feels like a huge, oily, dirty black ocean churning and splashing in me, disintegrating my wholeness and self-worth.'
- 'It sweeps over my head; the negative self-talk is black and ugly and takes over all rational thinking.'

Once you've explored what the shadow looks and feels like in your body, take a few minutes to breathe into this part of you. As you breathe in, imagine that pure oxygen is arriving at the shadow, almost greeting it like an old friend. See if you can imagine each breath softening or soothing the shadow. Notice what happens to the shadow when you do this. Does the shadow change shape? Does sensation dissipate?

Here's what happened when people in my community sent their breath towards the shadow as a way of welcoming and soothing it.

- 'The cold blue feeling diffused like clouds disappearing into the sky.'
- 'The dark sphere in my chest lightened in heaviness and reduced in size.'
- 'I saw a scared young girl who just wants to be accepted for who she is.'
- 'The tornado slowed, its intensity lessened and eventually, it turned into a puff of wind.'
- 'My shoulders dropped, and the tension melted away. The sensations were still there, but I wasn't suffering from them.'
- 'The cloak dissolved and disappeared. I connected with my personal power.'
- 'The heaviness lifted, and I could begin to hear the other, more supportive voice that lives within me.'
- 'When I offered the oily, dirty black ocean my breath it calmed down. The shadow loosened its grip. Space was created between my true self and the shadow's story.'

These responses, whilst diverse, all reveal the possibility that when we offer the shadows our non-judgemental awareness and our breath, sensation changes and we have greater capacity to unhook. From here, it's possible to connect with the deeper, more whole aspects of ourselves.

STEP THREE - BE HONEST

After identifying our shadows and exploring their felt expression within our bodies, it's time to get radically honest. Grab your notebook or journal and respond to these four questions:

1.   When I am caught up in this shadow, how do I feel about myself?
2.   What actions do I take?
3.   What do I miss out on when I'm believing/over-identifying with this shadow aspect of myself?
4.   What function does this shadow perform? How is it keeping me safe?

In my research group, people shared how their shadows made them feel: defective, insignificant, ashamed, frightened, overwhelmed, separate, incapable, inferior, defeated or broken.

In many cases, when people were caught up in the shadow energy, they took less care of themselves and acted in ways that didn't feel healthy or aligned. Respondents reported eating more unhealthy food, hitting the snooze button rather than exercising, meditating or doing yoga, snacking at night, scrolling social media for hours and making unnecessary purchases online. People also reported not speaking up in work meetings, actively hiding parts of themselves with others, lying or avoiding telling the truth.

Can you relate to any of these experiences? What do you do when pulled in by your shadows?

STEP FOUR -
ACCESS A DEEPER TRUTH

Now that we have softened the shadow, it's possible to communicate with it and potentially access some wisdom or a deeper truth. This step requires courage, honesty and a willingness to see ourselves and our lives in new ways.

You can open the lines of communication by asking your shadow the following questions (in any order):

- What do you need from me?
- How can I support you?
- What message do you have for me?
- What are you here to teach me?

In my community, people's shadows asked them for:

- Compassion and understanding.
- To be seen and heard.
- Unconditional love.
- More time being creative.
- Rest.

When opening to a deeper truth, people learnt that it was time to:

- Stop valuing the opinion of others above their own.
- Advocate for themselves.
- Not take on people's opinions of them.
- Realign their lives towards their values.

THEY DANCED WITH

CURIOSITY AND COMPASSION

BETWEEN THE SMALLER, YOUNGER ASPECTS OF THEMSELVES

AND THE DEEPER, WISER, INNER DIMENSIONS

- Come back to the basics of good food, exercise, meditation and journalling.
- Receive the support of family and friends.
- Pursue creative endeavours.
- Speak from the heart.
- Forge new friendships.
- Be brave and live more purposefully.

It was a delight for me to witness people from all around the world make this process their own as they opened the lines of communication between their shadows and their deeper selves. Community members asked their shadows what they needed. They soothed these parts of themselves - hugged them, held them, listened. They wrote letters of compassion and understanding.

They danced with curiosity and compassion between the smaller, younger parts of themselves and the deeper, wiser inner aspects. They deconditioned the habits of shame and aversion and moved towards wholehearted confidence, the willingness to be with, and learn from, the parts of themselves they often resist or hide.

WHY IS IT WORTH DOING THE WORK?

The *dancing with your shadows* framework outlined above might seem like a lot of work to you - I get it! Maybe you don't feel like getting to know your version of 'Doubting Deb' or 'Anna Anxiety'. Perhaps feeling like there's a tornado swirling around in your body doesn't appeal to you either. Sure, we'd all prefer to be given one affirmation, which after repeating a few times in the shower will magically erase our insecurities, doubts and fears of not being enough. Or maybe you are secretly hoping that the pretty yearly planner you bought with the inspirational comments will be enough to shift the way you feel about yourself?

Deep down, we all know that those superficial practices (and pretty stationery!) don't offer lasting transformation. Learning that you don't need to resist or be afraid of your shadows is an incredible gift you can give yourself. So, if you skipped over that section, consider going back and exploring it now. You'll be pleased you did!

I love the way Rose (the woman who is now, after forty years, painting animals and people again) described the process. She reflected:

> *'I've been doing self-improvement programs since I was a teenager, that's more than four decades. In almost every program I've tried, you are supposed to take an aspect of yourself and rip it off like a strip of bark or duct tape. There - all better, it's gone! How much more sensible is it to turn that aspect into a teacher and integrate it into your being?'*

Within my research, the majority of respondents discovered that their shadows developed when they were young as a way to keep them safe. Their shadows shielded them from being rejected by family or friends,

HOLD ME IN YOUR AWARENESS
WITH CURIOSITY AND COMPASSION
SO THAT I MAY WHISPER TO YOU
WHY I AM HERE
AND IN THE GENTLE ACT OF BEING HEARD
I CAN SOFTEN
SO YOU CAN SEE
WHO YOU REALLY ARE

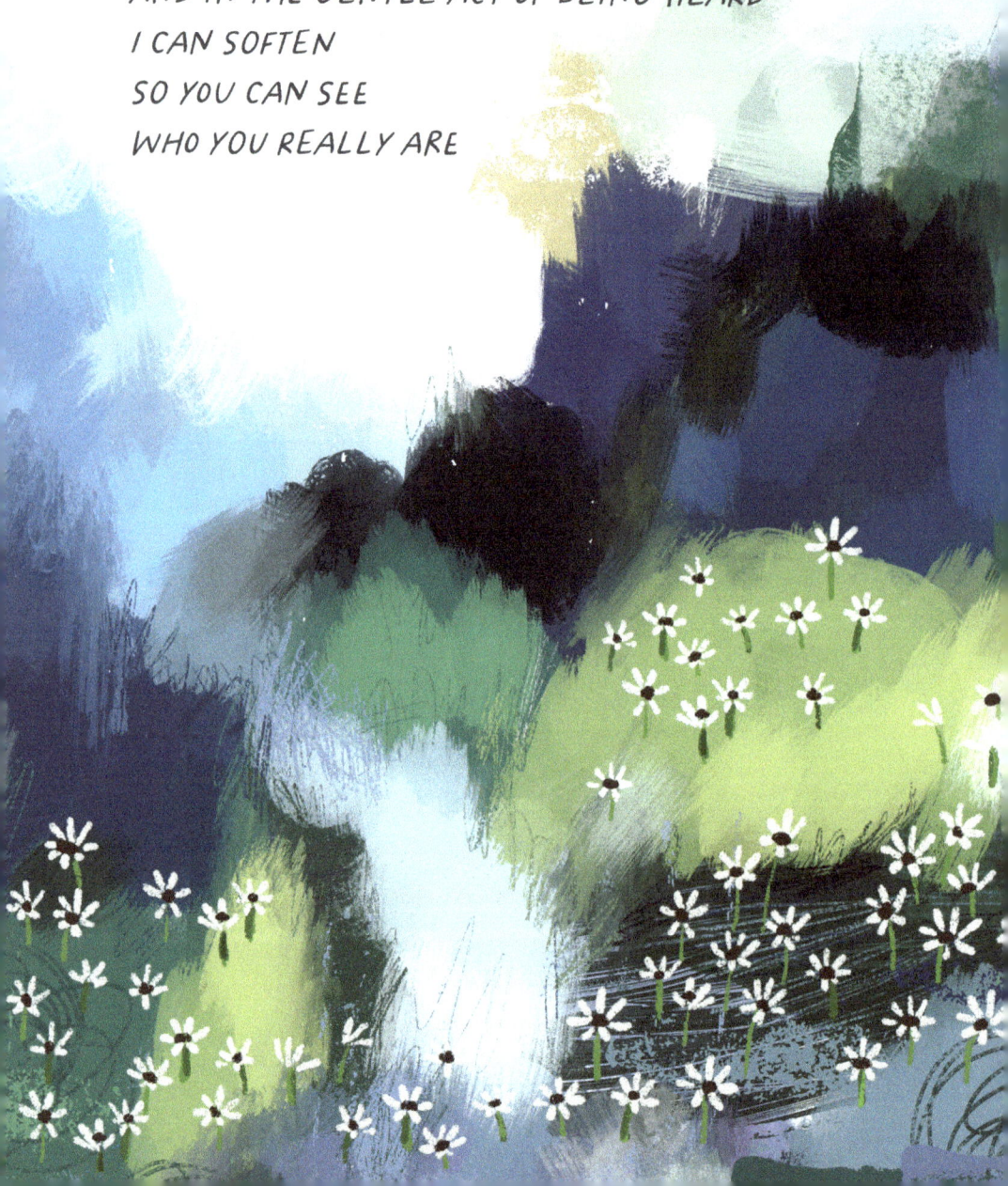

judged harshly, told they were too much or unlovable, yelled at or exposed for not being clever enough.

They put the needs of their parents above their own so as not to rock the boat, especially in family environments that felt unstable. They worked hard to desperately prove that they were as intelligent as their sister or brother. They developed a narrative that if they were perfect, then they would receive love, if they were invisible, then they wouldn't get hurt (physically or emotionally).

Whilst well intentioned, our shadows can stop us from evolving and moving forward. They can also prevent us from loving and receiving love, taking risks and achieving our full potential.

When community members reflected upon what they missed out on when they were over-identifying with their shadows, the most common theme related to human connection and belonging. People turned down offers to have lunch with colleagues and to go out with friends on the weekends. When they did go out, they were distracted. As George commented, 'The fear of being judged and my loud inner critic acted as a distracting, static noise during interactions with others.'

People also felt less inclined to speak from the heart or have honest conversations about their needs, opinions and wants. For many, this led to feelings of loneliness and separation.

If we want to feel whole, experience deep human connection and a sense of belonging, we need to be brave enough to take our shadows by the hand. When we do, we get a more complete understanding of who we are. We learn how to transform our fears and wounded aspects into hope, courage and confidence.

In the next section, we'll go over each of the three shadows in more detail. Even if you don't identify with each shadow now it's still worth a read, as you might find it appears in your future or it impacts your friends, your partner or your children. You might even smile as you begin to understand someone you are close to in a new way.

SHADOW ONE - NOT ENOUGHNESS

We live in a culture of scarcity that encourages us to see ourselves, our relationships and our lives from the lens of 'not enough'. We turn this scarcity strobe both inwards and outwards. When focused on inward scarcity, we tell ourselves we aren't attractive, slim or fit enough. We reprimand ourselves for not being productive, driven, organised or purposeful enough. We worry that we aren't interesting, kind, funny, compassionate or patient enough.

Outward scarcity sees us comparing ourselves to others and feeling less than. We see other people's success or happiness and subconsciously fear there isn't enough to go around - enough success, money, love, satisfaction or happiness.

To better understand how this shadow plays out for you, reflect on these three questions.

1. Do I relate most strongly to the inward or outward scarcity lens?

2. What are my most common not enough stories or beliefs that play on repeat in my mind?

3. In what situations do I experience not enoughness? (For example, at work, home, socially, after the fact as I lay in bed at night, before the event.)

INTERNAL SCARCITY

PHYSICALITY	PERSONALITY	LIFE STAGE	RELATIONSHIPS
Not slim enough	Not interesting enough	Not successful enough	Not loved enough
Not attractive enough	Not funny enough	Not satisfied enough	Not valued enough
Not fit enough	Not patient enough	Not purposeful enough	Not respected nough
Not toned enough	Not kind enough	Not established enough	Not appreciated enough
Not tall enough	Not clever enough	Not mature enough	Not popular enough

EXTERNAL SCARCITY

OTHER PEOPLE	LIFE
Other people are more successful than me.	There isn't enough success for all of us.
Other people's lives are more interesting, rewarding, exciting than mine.	There's isn't enough love for us all to be happy.
Other people have more money, love, success, opportunity than me.	There isn't enough time for me to achieve everything I want to.

Seeing ourselves, our relationships and our lives through the lens of scarcity has a profound impact on our thoughts. It's like we are listening to the same Spotify playlist day in, day out. With melodies of shame and a chorus of self-aversion, these songs are a combination of comforting in their familiarity and damaging in their effect.

Over time, we find ourselves in what world-renowned meditation teacher and psychologist Tara Brach refers to as the 'trance of unworthiness' - feeling that we are deeply flawed, not worthy of love, happiness, success or approval.

Given these conversations occur within our own minds and are private, it's illuminating to get a window into other people's inner dialogue. My meditation community shared the exact words that played on repeat in their mind, day after day. For example:

- 'There's something wrong with you.'
- 'You will fail so don't bother trying.'
- 'You should just quit.'
- 'You never do anything right.'
- 'You always do the wrong thing.'
- 'I'm not important.'
- 'I don't know how to make friends.'
- 'I don't deserve to have friends that I look up to.'
- 'You are lazy.'
- 'You never accomplish anything.'
- 'You don't know what you want.'
- 'You are unreliable.'

Their voice of inner doubt asked rhetorical questions on a loop too. Questions like:

- 'What is wrong with you?'
- 'Why would anyone like you?'
- 'Why would anyone take you seriously?'
- 'What if I'm not interesting?'
- 'What if I can't do it?'

Thoughts are more than just words that populate our minds. They impact our physical and emotional bodies, shimmering through every cell. Respondents commented on how these thoughts made their bodies feel heavy, contracted, achy, tight and sore. When these thoughts were left attended, respondents felt incapable, ashamed, defective and insignificant.

As their bodies closed off and their emotional world became heavy, they missed opportunities for deep and meaningful connections. Missed opportunities included:

- The chance to be fully present and to speak from the heart.
- The possibility of really finding their people through authenticity and genuine connection.
- Exploring new interests and hobbies.
- A sense of satisfaction at what they had accomplished.
- Feeling at ease in their own bodies.
- Starting their day feeling calm and peaceful.
- Ending the day feeling satisfied and at ease.

In some people, there was an unbearable loneliness that emerged from over-identifying with the shadow of not enough. All these experiences support a key premise of Brené Brown's qualitative research on shame, vulnerability and courage - the culture of scarcity leads to disconnection.

I TAKE MY
YOUNGER HAND
AND TOGETHER
WE WALK

CONFIDENCE IN ACTION - MY VOICE MATTERS

Lisa grew up in a household where her father drank too much and was prone to outbursts of rage. Her younger brother also directed violence towards her, one time chasing her with an axe.

'My mother had no idea what to do, so she just stayed quiet,' explained Lisa. As a young girl, she internalised these experiences and grew up believing that she wasn't worth protecting.

Lisa went on to accomplish much in her adult life. She was a journalist, a published novelist, a teacher of English to immigrants and a mother to two amazing daughters. But, despite her achievements, she always felt a sense of unworthiness. She spent her adult life keeping her opinions (and needs) to herself. She deferred to what others wanted as a way of ensuring they didn't get angry with her. For Lisa, this was a hard way to live.

Lisa embraced the opportunity to explore her shadow of self-doubt. She reflected upon how this shadow appeared most frequently in her relationships with men.

She shared, 'It appears frequently in my marriage; it haunts my relationship with my brother; it has been present in every love relationship I've ever had. It comes whenever I must talk to a man I am close to about my own wants, needs, opinions, beliefs, etc. It has been around for as long as I can remember.'

For Lisa, this shadow expressed itself as agitation throughout her body – a jitteriness, like discordant notes being played on a piano. When Lisa over-identified with this shadow, she felt everything from anxious to self-loathing – flawed, insufficient and less than.

'When I am caught up in this shadow, I often avoid telling the truth, sometimes I even lie,' she says. 'Because I am so afraid that if I speak the truth, whatever man it is I'm speaking to will get angry or stop loving me.'

Through meditation, journalling and quiet reflection, Lisa discovered that this shadow's initial intention was to keep her safe in a volatile family home whilst growing up. By keeping her quiet, by not asserting herself, this shadow ensured that she wouldn't do anything that might draw the anger or attention of others.

Lisa has spent a lifetime deferring her own needs and desires in order to please her father, brother, boyfriend and husband. After working through this four-part process, she realised that her shadow of self-doubt was more than just a protective mechanism, it also had a deeper message for her.

It wanted her to know that she has a voice. She commented, 'The idea that my wants and needs matter as much as anyone else's is revolutionary for me. It's not just speaking up for myself that I am learning, it's also that I deserve to have someone speak up for me, and that this person should be me!'

Can you identify with Lisa's experience of deferring her own needs and desires so as to please others? What small step could you take towards expressing your own needs this week?

I am enough
I am worthy
I am safe
I am loveable

I choose a new story

MINDFUL PRACTICE
I AM ENOUGH

As always, begin with a few breaths in the wholehearted posture. Imagine a smile shining down on you. Feel it soften your body. Relax your shoulders and open your heart. Offer this smile to the earth beneath you.

Picture a time over the last week or so when you felt like you weren't enough. Bring the details to mind. Were you at home, at work, on social media, lying in bed at night? Did it relate to a relationship or role you perform, as a parent, child, friend or colleague?

Focus once more on the wholehearted posture and on any feelings of openness and receptivity. From this expanded state, reflect on these three questions:

1. When I'm caught in the energy of not enough, what actions do I take or not take?
2. When my focus is on not feeling enough, what opportunities or experiences do I miss out on?
3. What is this shadow trying to protect me from?

If you feel comfortable, thank this shadow and then offer it some soothing words or phrases, or anything else it needs to feel seen and heard.

Finish this reflection by placing a hand on your heart (or chest) and whispering to yourself: *I am enough.*

SAME WOUND, DIFFERENT BEHAVIOUR

It's easy to assume, when we are caught up over-identifying with the shadow of not enough, that we will shrink and make ourselves smaller so as not to offend, disappoint or aggravate others.

This shadow can, however, also have the opposite effect. Our deep fear of not being worthy can express itself as being the life of the party, the funny friend, the leader of the parent committee or the person who organises all the social gatherings at work.

Perhaps you can think of someone who responds to their not enoughness in these more outward ways? Maybe it's you! It's important to note that neither strategy (making ourselves smaller or bigger) is better or worse, they are just different coping mechanisms stemming from the same core wound or shadow.

And of course, the irony is that the definition of confidence we are taught to aspire towards - that of holding people's attention, taking on leadership roles in all different aspects of life and always feeling self-assured - may be a shiny veneer hiding a darker, more wobbly truth.

One of my community members, Rob, explains the relationship he has with 'Charlie', his shadow. It's a powerful reminder of just how creative we can be when attempting to soothe our primal need for acceptance, safety and belonging.

CONFIDENCE IN ACTION -
NUMB & EXHILARATED

Rob grew up feeling shy, lonely and different to his family. As a child, he didn't feel safe, nurtured or reassured. His mother was emotionally frail, scared of the world and needy. His father was stern, emotionally unavailable and sometimes physically abusive. Neither parent provided Rob with a sense of safety or love. Nor did they offer any helpful preparation for life.

Rob survived his loneliness by believing at an early age that there was something out there for him - God, source, supreme being, a higher force watching over him. As a child, he would connect to this godlike source feeling of white light. This was years before he learnt about meditation.

Rob's reflection on developing a spiritual practice at an early age reminded me of my own rituals as a child. Growing up, I had a special place on a cliff that looked out across a wild expanse of ocean. As far as my little eyes could see, deep, dark blue ocean. I would sit on that cliff top and feel small yet deeply connected to all life. Like Rob, I too connected to a loving energy that helped me feel safe and like I belonged to something bigger.

I'm curious, did you have any little rituals or habits as a child that now you can see were the beginnings of your spiritual practice?

In response to feeling anxious as a child and uncomfortable as a teenager in social situations, Rob created 'Charlie'. He reflects, 'Charlie was born to help me cope in social situations. He first appeared in middle school as I navigated the discomfort of social events and high school parties.

Charlie is
like the wind,
always moving,
changing
speeds and
impacting the
environment.

Internally there's a dual feeling of
numbness and exhileration

Charlie helped me feel safe by releasing my self-doubt and allowing me to care less about what others thought of me. This offered great freedom from social fears and adolescent insecurities.'

Whilst exploring wholehearted confidence and this framework for being with our shadows, Rob reflected on his relationship with Charlie over the years. He shared how, when he was young, Charlie felt freeing, giving him permission to be different and to find his comfort in discomfort.

As an adult, however, with responsibilities and consequences for his actions, Charlie often led Rob down a path that created pain for himself and others.

With age, greater awareness and understanding, Rob has distanced himself from Charlie and learnt to find more peace and joy in his life. He no longer needs to manufacture thrills with Charlie as a means of feeling alive and valued.

Rob reflected, 'Knowing that I can live with Charlie and learn from what he has been trying to teach me has been one of the greatest lessons of my life.'

I'm curious, how do you respond to your shadow of not enough or to the feelings of self-doubt? Do you shrink, moulding yourself into a version of you that won't upset others? Or do you become larger than life, using humour, or overcompensating by taking on extra roles and responsibilities at work or in your community?

Next time you notice yourself acting in these ways, pause, feel it in your body and get curious about how you could soothe this shadow and step into your deeper, more confident expression.

SHADOW - IMPOSTER SYNDROME

Take a moment to reflect on these questions:

- When people offer you praise at work, do you have trouble trusting it?
- Do you sometimes feel like if people knew the 'real you' they wouldn't respect or like you as much?
- Do you fear you'll be found out?
- Do stories like, *When I have more experience, then I'll be the real deal*, swirl around in your mind?
- When you must work hard to get results, does it make you feel like you aren't clever or up to the task at hand?

If you answered yes to any of these questions, you are probably like 70% of the population who have also experienced imposter syndrome at some stage in their lives.

The term was first coined by psychologists Dr Clance and Dr Imes in 1978. In their article, titled *The Impostor Phenomenon in High Achieving Women: Dynamics and Therapeutic Intervention*, they describe the key features as: a habit of attributing achievement to luck or timing, a disconnect between external praise and internal feelings, and a fear of being found out.

Whilst their research was based on the experience of women, it's widely acknowledged today that this psychological phenomenon effects men, women, members of the LGBTQI+ community and people in minority groups.

Given our interest in exploring the childhood context of our shadows, let's take some time to understand the two key family experiences that contributed to imposter syndrome for the women in Dr Clance and Dr Imes' research.

Childhood environment one: Growing up in a family where their sibling or close relative was designated as the 'intelligent' one and they were deemed sensitive, socially unskilled or not intelligent.

For these women, they received the message that no matter what they accomplished, they would never prove themselves to be as clever as their sibling. Part of them believed this narrative, but the other part desperately wanted to disprove it. These women went on to succeed at school but didn't receive the recognition at home. From here, the unhealthy tug of war between achieving real success and also feeling like she will never be enough carried into adulthood.

Childhood environment two: Being told as a child that they were superior in every way. These girls received consistent messages that there was nothing they couldn't do if they wanted to, and that they could also do it with ease.

As these young girls grew, they realised that they could not do everything they wanted to, and that some things were difficult to achieve. Yet, they felt obligated to their family to keep up the facade of 'perfection with ease'. Over time, when they had to work hard for good grades, they jumped to the conclusion that they must be dumb. As Dr Clane and Dr Imes state, 'She is not a genius; therefore, she must be an intellectual impostor.'

Given that these findings are over forty years old and only explore the experience of women, it's worth noting that these will not be the only two family dynamics that may encourage imposter syndrome. If you're curious about how your childhood may have contributed to this shadow, set some time aside and reflect on these questions:

- Growing up, was there someone who was deemed 'the clever one'? If so, who was it? What impact did this have on you as a child?

- Did your parents or carers make comparisons between you and your siblings? If so, what were they and how did they make you feel?

- When you 'achieved' as a child (academically, at sport, drama or music) did it feel wholesome, or was there a feeling of stress or expectations tied to this?

CONVERSATIONS THAT NURTURE RATHER THAN DEFINE

If you are a parent, grandparent or have anything to do with young people, you might be starting to feel a rumbling of guilt, regret or worry inside as you reflect upon all the ways you may have negatively affected your children or the young people who've entered your life.

Maybe you are picturing a particular conversation when you said something that you now regret, or a way you supported your kids during high school that whilst well intentioned, now feels inappropriate? When we reflect on our own childhood (and the impact it has had on our adult selves), it's natural to start to wonder about all the ways we ourselves may have failed others.

So, before you rush out and buy all the parenting books, or offer to pay for your adult children's therapy, let's take a moment to reflect on the ways that wholehearted confidence can help us engage with young people in more mindful, compassionate and wise ways.

Let's begin with a powerful (and reassuring) suggestion from Brené Brown, in her book *Daring Greatly:*

> 'Who we are and how we engage with the world are much stronger predictors of how our children will do than what we know about parenting. The question isn't "Are you parenting the right way?" it's "Are you the adult that you want your child to grow up to be?" '

The good news is that, as you move through this book and learn how to embrace and learn from your vulnerabilities, live from your values, lean into your own inherent goodness and trust in life, you will, by way of modelling, be teaching your children or other young people to do the same.

And if your children are older, you could practise forgiveness of your younger self, or have an honest conversation with your adult children about your past parenting choices and how you feel about them. If this broad-brush stroke of reassurance isn't enough to soothe the inner rumblings, here are seven ways you can show up and support children wholeheartedly today.

1. **Openly share the mistakes you have made**. Communicate how you are moving forward, either through self-forgiveness, making amends or taking responsibility for your actions. Encourage children to understand that mistakes are a natural part of life and do not mean that you are not worthy or enough.

2. **Praise effort not outcome.** When encouraging and supporting children, focus your attention on qualities that relate to effort, like perseverance, creativity, conceptual thinking, courage or commitment rather than on test scores, grades or outcomes.

3. **Take the time to identify your values as a family.** Include your children in the process. Use your family values to guide family decision-making, to help your kids in challenging times and as conversation starters at dinner etc.

4. **Be mindful.** Carve out time each day to put your phone down and really listen to your children or young people with all your senses. Notice facial expressions and the emotion that lives underneath the words. Connect with their needs in the moment, to feel seen, heard and recognised. Allow for moments of silence so that these young people can come up with their own solutions rather than you offering advice.

5. **Practise what you preach.** If you want your kids to have downtime without technology before bed, make sure you do too. If you want your kids to forgive themselves and practise self-compassion, actively model this for your children also. If you desire for your kids to stop sweating the small stuff, make an effort not to get stressed when you burn the dinner or run late for a dentist appointment.

6. **Enjoy things regardless of skill.** Take an art class, join a sports team, let your children or the young people in your life see that you can have fun and enjoy yourself even when you aren't the best.

7. **Support young people to embrace and learn from their insecurities or shadows**. Remind them that they can dream big, be in the school play or try out for the soccer team even when that little voice in their head tells them not to. Use this exact framework to support young people to take risks and try new things even when they feel nervous or uncomfortable. Children are inherently creative, so you might be surprised and delighted at how easily they engage with it.

CONFIDENCE IN ACTION - DO YOU HAVE CHEMISTRY?

George lives in America. He has been a member of my meditation community since the beginning. His commitment to understanding himself and remembering his deeper nature is inspiring. Never missing a weekly meditation, attending Zooms at three in the morning, always curious, forever willing to bring a sense of humour to what can sometimes feel like heavy work.

During George's childhood, his mother frequently told him that he was clever. 'This built up my self-esteem but from a sense of being superior to others', he explained. When George explored this shadow, a scene from high school surfaced as if it were yesterday. He recalled how his teacher loved to return the chemistry tests in a stack at the front of the classroom. They were arranged in ascending order such that others had to go through the lowest scoring students to get to their test. George shared, 'Needless to say, it was easy for me to find my test.'

After receiving another poor score on a test, George spent the night reviewing where he had gone wrong. He discovered an error in the teacher's grading, and felt confident that if he showed his teacher, he could increase his test score. The next day George plucked up the courage and approached his teacher. The conversation didn't go as he expected or hoped. George did not receive the credit. And even more damaging to his young psyche was that he felt misunderstood and let down by his teacher who was not willing to see his point of view.

Whilst exploring wholehearted confidence, George realised his experiences in high school chemistry contributed mightily to the imposter syndrome he has experienced for most of his career.

He shared, 'I learned that at any moment I could have it all swept out from under me. This enabled my inner critic to take charge as a means of self-protection. The inner critic rationalised that harassing me for my mistakes meant that others' criticism would pale in comparison and so I wouldn't be hurt by them. I compensated by spending more time working. I held the belief that some people will be smarter than me, but I will work harder than them.'

Over the years, George passed up offers to go to lunch with his colleagues, instead, he ate at his desk and worked through. As a result, he didn't make any friends and missed that energising, enriching aspect of his work life. George also remembers freezing in work meetings and planning his responses with such detail that by the time he was ready to contribute, people had moved onto another topic.

The imposter syndrome meant George worked long hours and on the weekends. It took time away from his family and put strain on his marriage. He also missed out on other pleasurable pursuits like creative writing.

BEFRIEND

In the spirit of wholehearted confidence, rather than eradicating this shadow, George has totally changed his relationship with it. It no longer pulls him in or casts a darkness over other areas of his life. George now makes time for creative pursuits, like poetry. In fact, he has used poetry to break free from this shadow, and to hold it in a more loving, creative container of awareness. Funny, George has no imposter syndrome when sharing this poem!

OUT OF FEAR

Purposely and methodically choosing to miss out,
the overly protective, misguided guardian.
From cowering under imposed self-discipline,
to being held by self-compassion.
Unfurling resolve to protect what matters most,
snuggled in arms of love
smuggled past the clutches of fear.
Past the bracing defense against anxiety's expectation
of humiliating laughter at not knowing the answer.
To joyously embracing laughing at oneself,
for finally being found out.
Found out for being human.
Found out for having questions.
Found out for having purpose.
To finally venture out,
for there is everything to love
on the widening path to becoming whole.

George

MINDFUL PRACTICE
I HAVE NOTHING TO HIDE

Sit in the wholehearted posture. Take a few deep breaths. Imagine that the energy of a smile is travelling down from the sky into your body and then into the earth below.

Cast your mind back to a time recently when you experienced imposter syndrome.

Reflect upon where you were, what you were doing, the type of thoughts you were having, what your posture felt like.

See if you can locate this shadow somewhere in your body. Do you feel it in your chest, gut, heart or back? Does it feel heavy, dull, sharp, tight?

Take a few deep breaths and see if you can soften any sensations.

Reflect upon these three questions:

1. When I'm caught up in this shadow, what do I miss out on?
2. What does this shadow aspect of me need?
3. What have I learnt about myself by exploring my imposter syndrome?

You may like to finish this practice by offering yourself, or your shadow, a soothing phrase like: *Thank you for trying to protect me, but I'm strong enough to take risks and try new things. I have nothing to hide.*

SHADOW - HIGH EXPECTATIONS

When I reflect upon my own shadow of high expectations, two stories, thirteen years apart, come to mind. The first occurred about fifteen years ago. My first son was eight months old, and like many new mothers, the transition from working professional to stay-at-home mum was presenting its challenges.

With the value of hindsight, I brought the self-imposed high expectations I had in relation to work into my role as a mother (same wound, different playground!).

Desperate and determined to be perfect at my new and most important role yet, I created a strict mental list of dos and don'ts. Rather than seeing these as guiding principles or good intentions, I turned them into objective truths. For example, as a 'good mother' I will always attend to my child's needs above my own. I will do the washing and tidy the kitchen before resting. I will serve only home-cooked meals. I will read at least three bedtime stories per night. (I'm pleased to say I stopped short of putting lipstick on before my husband came home from work, which was indeed an expectation of many women in past generations.)

The mental list went on and on until I found myself locked in a prison of my own making.

As I continually measured myself against these impossible expectations, my self-confidence eroded. Keen for a new way to live, I went to see a psychologist. Within about ten minutes, she asked me if I would ever consider buying takeaway for dinner. To which I exclaimed in horror, 'No, of course not!' The underlying belief behind my strong reaction - good mothers don't buy packaged food, they cook everything from scratch.

At the time, I was so hooked into this belief that there was no space to entertain any other possibilities. Seeing the whole conversation with the psychologist as nonsense and not worth my time or money, I never returned. Can you guess what I did with the extra time - I steamed chicken and vegetables!

I look back on that conversation and can now see that the psychologist was trying to create some space between me and my self-imposed high expectations. But between the sleepless nights, unpredictable routine and rumbling anxiety, I just couldn't see my ideas as anything but cold, hard facts. That's what stress does to us — narrows our outlook and makes us cling onto our ideas of right and wrong.

A few years, and hundreds of home-cooked meals later (many of which were thrown on the floor), I was introduced to the idea of the 'good enough mother'. First coined in 1953 by Donald Winnicott, a British pediatrician and psychoanalyst, the theory of the good enough mother acknowledges that there comes a time in a child's development when they benefit when their mothers fail them in small ways (please note: I'm not talking about neglect or abuse).

Obviously, when babies are first born, it's important to respond to their needs immediately so that they feel safe and cared for. But as the months and years progress, being failed in *small and tolerable ways* helps children prepare for life in an imperfect world.

As mothers, fathers or caregivers, every time we ask our children to leave the playground before they want to, every time we are unable to give them our undivided attention, every time we ask them to share with their siblings, we are preparing them to survive in a society that will disappoint and frustrate them. When children have these lessons in a safe and supportive family environment, they build trust that even when life doesn't go their way, they will still be okay.

Understanding that I didn't need to be a perfect mother to raise a happy and resilient child was a huge light-bulb moment for me. It enabled me to begin the long (and continuous) process of softening my expectations.

Perhaps you are a parent, grandparent or caregiver and this story has enabled you to see your own self-imposed high expectations with wider eyes? Maybe there is another role you perform as a colleague, manager, friend, sibling, child or carer that you could explore in relation to your high expectations?

As you begin to get curious, it's important to remind ourselves that the good enough mother, the good enough colleague, friend or child, is a gift to both you and the other person in the relationship. We all benefit when we accept the imperfect nature of relationships.

WRITING PRACTICE
FROM PERFECT TO
GOOD ENOUGH

Set aside ten to fifteen minutes. Trust that this will be time well spent. Identify a role you are currently performing that you can sense is causing you some stress, overwhelm or concern. Perhaps there is a role you ruminate about when lying in bed at night. Maybe there is a role that takes up a lot of your energy and you often feel like you have fallen short.

With this role in mind, divide your page and write two headings that make sense to you. For example, the 'perfect parent' and the 'good enough parent'. The 'perfect friend' and the 'good enough friend'.

Take five minutes to populate the first column. Write down all the expectations, beliefs and rules you have about this role. The sillier the better! When we can smile at how ridiculous some of these are, we create space for change.

Read over the list and notice how it makes you feel in your body. Ask yourself: *When I am caught up believing this list, how do I feel about myself? What do I miss out on?*

Take another five minutes to populate the second column. With kindness and compassion, explore what being good enough might look and feel like. As you do this, keep in mind the idea that the good enough relationship benefits both you and the other person.

Read over the second list. Notice how it makes you feel in your heart. You might sense relief, fear, vulnerability, sadness or love. Remind yourself that this is a process and that it's allowed to feel messy.

Ask yourself the following questions:

- How could I support myself to really live from this second list each day?
- What does the younger part of me need as I make the transition from perfect to good enough?
- What does my adult self need?

You can do this activity with different roles you play at work or at home. Trust that over time you will begin to soften those self-imposed high expectations and as a consequence, feel more self-accepting, assured and free.

CONFIDENCE IN ACTION - AN UGLY SMUDGE ON A BEAUTIFUL DAY

Isobel is an outgoing person who enjoys being sociable. She likes meeting new people and embracing challenges that push her to take risks or be the centre of attention.

On the outside, she appears self-assured. During this process of understanding her shadows, Isobel realised that when she is out and about being sociable, she feels confident, but when she gets home, she becomes pulled into the habits of rumination and replaying the event in her mind. It's these mental habits that cause her confidence to erode.

Shortly after starting a new job, Isobel went to a workplace barbecue. She had a wonderful time meeting new people. Everyone was friendly and she had great conversations. In the moment, she felt happy, engaged and present. When she returned home, she told her husband what a wonderful time she had.

Later that night, as she lay in bed, the shadow of high expectations appeared. It started pointing out all the things she 'screwed up'. Tiny details, like how she spoke over someone or forgot to introduce someone, or made a joke that in retrospect might have been misunderstood or offensive.

Isobel reflected on the impact of this shadow. 'I picture it like a bunch of big ugly smudges on what was a beautiful day,' she said, 'I feel it in my gut, kind of like nausea. It makes me want to curl up and hide. I feel embarrassed and stupid. It sucks, because these big ugly smudges overtake the memory of what was a wonderful day and transform it into something else.'

As Isobel engaged with the wholehearted confidence process, exploring how this shadow felt in her body and the wisdom it held, she realised it was there to remind her that connecting with people and being social are important aspects of her life. She received the message that it's okay to want to be good at it, but it doesn't need to make her feel miserable.

This shadow helped Isobel to remember that silly slips in social situations are normal and they just mean she is human. She reflected, 'Seeing my shadow as an ally is a relief. It feels less heavy and negative. When I treat my shadow with compassion, it feels like I'm treating myself with compassion also, which is always helpful. Seeing it all with a sense of humour is useful too.'

I'm curious - do you lie in bed at night replaying conversations, wishing you had said something differently? Do you ruminate on small mistakes? How can Isobel's story inspire you to offer yourself compassion in these moments? Or could a healthy dose of humour and perspective be your soothing balm?

THE GOOD ENOUGH AUTHOR

Now for my second story. About thirteen years after my good enough mother realisation, I drove to the post office to collect a box of my first book, *Ten Pathways*. In honesty, writing about my experience of living with chronic pain required a level of vulnerability I hadn't anticipated. Every chapter revealed deeper layers of my conditioned identity crying out to be witnessed. The writing process was challenging, illuminating and liberating all at once.

That's why on this day, driving to the post office, I felt so relieved. I had created a neat little story that holding my book was going to be a line in the sand moment for me. No more mess. Healing complete. One giant tick beside that chapter of my life. I remember feeling so happy that I was singing in the car. It was like a scene from a feel-good movie about a middle-aged woman finding herself.

I couldn't wait to get home to open the box of books. So, I stood in the car park, used my house key to cut through the tape, and ripped open the box. I pulled out a book and felt the smooth cover on my palm. The satisfaction and relief were palpable. My shoulders dropped. I smiled and sighed at the same time. I opened the book and was immediately greeted with a typo in large font on the first page. The momentary wave of relief was replaced with disappointment. I could tell it came from a very young part of me.

Once I'd moved through the surface emotions of disbelief, frustration and blame, I got in touch with something deeper. I realised that within this moment there was an invitation. I was being asked to be a 'good enough author'! Life was presenting me with an opportunity to like myself, and my book, even amidst the imperfections.

So, that afternoon I hand-delivered copies of my book to my closest family, friends and colleagues. It was both a real and symbolic gesture. Love me. Accept me. Even when I am not perfect. And of course, these moments felt more raw and beautiful because of my vulnerability.

Perhaps you can think back to a moment like this in your own life? A time when you had to present something like a birthday cake, Christmas dinner or work presentation in a way that didn't meet your own self-imposed high expectations or definition of perfection? Perhaps your kids didn't even notice the crooked birthday cake? Maybe family and friends felt more relaxed eating a meal that revealed your humanness? Was it only you who thought that work presentation could have been better?

I shared those two stories to remind you of a key theme on the wholehearted confidence journey – that of *welcoming*. We are not climbing a spiritual or personal development ladder where every rung represents an aspect of ourselves that we have overcome and risen above. We aren't striving to become recovering perfectionists. We are learning to see it all as a grand invitation to befriend our shadows and return to wholeness in big and small ways every day.

For me, my own growing experience of wholehearted confidence is evident in the contrast between the two stories. Sitting in the psychologist's room, the possibility that I could soften my own expectations was incomprehensible. Neither my mind nor heart was ready. The shadow was so opaque I couldn't see any way through it.

Over the years, with a continued commitment to exploring my inner world through meditation, mindfulness, curiosity and compassion, I

am now able to identify my shadows more quickly. I can sense their expression in my physical body. I find it easy to communicate with these aspects of myself. Even when it feels uncomfortable, I no longer squash them down or resist them. Instead, I enquire gently: *What would you have me know?* Usually the answer is simple: *You are enough just as you are.*

MAKING THE WHOLEHEARTED PATH YOUR OWN

As part two draws to a close, I hope you are feeling more confident in meeting the different aspects of yourself, including those inner dimensions you have habitually judged, criticised or resisted. But even more than this, I hope that you are learning to trust that you:

- know when to dive deep into your inner world, and when to have a break.
- get to make these practices feel supportive, safe and relevant for you.
- can be as creative as you like along the way.

The wholehearted confidence path isn't about strictly following my guidance, it's about combining my suggestions with your own wisdom. It was a delight for me to learn about all the different ways people in my community made this process of dancing with their shadows uniquely theirs.

Many people felt intuitively drawn to asking their shadows what they needed with the tenderness of a parent to a child. In their minds and in their hearts, they offered hugs, soothing phrases, reassurance and permission to leave. Others wrote to their shadows as a way to heal. People also carved out time for creative endeavours like drawing, painting and poetry. Some took up dancing classes. Others danced in their living rooms.

I love this letter that one community member wrote:

> 'Thank you, dear shadow. I know you love me and care deeply for my survival. I see you. I hear you. I understand you. I am sorry you are hurting. I do not need you to protect me with your story. It's actually not helping me. I am an adult now and I know my worth. You can trust me to look after us. I've been doing it for many years now, despite your best efforts. So, I am going to take my power back. You can hop in the backseat and buckle up, because you're welcome to come along for the ride but you do NOT get to drive. I love you. We are enough, always have been, always will be. These are the facts. Let's go.'

HOW FORGIVENESS REALLY FEELS

By trusting in their ability to make this process their own, many community members opened to the possibility of forgiveness. People shared how they were ready to let go of the resentment and anger they held towards the kids who bullied them at school. Others were able to see their now-elderly parents who had wronged them as children with compassion. People were able to forgive themselves for the mistakes they had made in the past. The bad choices and regrets were now only a small part of their life story, not the main act.

But let's be clear - the forgiveness they experienced wasn't about condoning the harmful actions of others or denying suffering or injustice. It was an invitation to let go of the contraction and weight that stems from resentment, blame, judgement, guilt and shame. It was an opportunity for people to experience a type of peace that comes from acceptance and compassion.

The process of forgiveness wasn't neat or linear. As with all human processes, there were mixed emotions, steps forward and then steps backwards. But underneath the messiness was a commitment to wholehearted confidence and our growing capacity to welcome it all. I hope you'll try this gentle forgiveness practice.

MINDFUL PRACTICE FORGIVENESS FOR YOU & ME

Spend a moment in the wholehearted posture.

Invite the energy of a smile to wash from the sky over you. Share this sense of openness and receptivity with the earth beneath you.

Allow someone you may have hurt, disappointed or let down to come to mind and heart. Breathe deeply. Repeat silently in your mind a few times: *I am sorry. Please forgive me.*

Stay with this practice for as long as you need. Notice emotions as they move through you. Be aware of physical sensations. Welcome it all.

Allow someone who has hurt, disappointed or let you down to come to mind and heart. Breathe deeply. Repeat silently in your mind a few times: *I forgive you.* (You may like to add any other phrases here too.) Again, allow emotions and sensations to come and go. Let it be imperfect or messy.

Finally, imagine that you are looking down upon yourself. Really see yourself sitting in this moment. Brave. Open. Forgiving.

Place your hand on your heart. Connect with your own heartbeat. Repeat silently in your mind: *I forgive myself.*

Allow the ways you have been unkind to yourself, the times you haven't lived up to your expectations to move in and out of your awareness like clouds in the sky. Let the smile in the sky hold the energy of forgiveness.

You can make this practice your own by developing phrases that resonate for you. You can do this practice at the end of the day as a way of letting go of the everyday regrets and disappointments. Or you could incorporate it into any of the shadow work. Developing the habit of self-forgiveness will help you connect with your deeper nature. Consistently forgiving others may also improve your relationships. Stay open and curious and be willing to be surprised.

PART TWO: SELF-REFLECTION

As we've learnt in part two, wholehearted confidence includes identifying, welcoming and learning from our humanness. I hope you've experienced, even if just for a moment at a time, how welcoming your shadows with curiosity, compassion and creativity can lead you to deeper truths and a growing experience of inner confidence.

Far from being something to avoid, resist or criticise, the different dimensions of our humanness have much to teach us.

When we learn to be with our shadows in these more wise and skilful ways, it also helps us to become more tolerant and understanding of other people's shadows. We'll explore how wholehearted confidence can improve our relationships in part three.

For now, take a moment to answer these three questions:

1. Which shadow is strongest in my life right now?
2. How can I support myself when I feel pulled in by this shadow?
3. How can I use creativity, forgiveness and compassion to break free?

YOUR CONFIDENCE COMMITMENTS

Repeat these phrases in the morning or at night, out loud or in your mind. Write them in your journal or on a Post-it Note. Use them any time you want to drop into the feeling of wholehearted confidence.

I am not afraid to explore my shadows.

I know how to access the wisdom contained within my vulnerabilities.

I remind myself that I am enough.

I have nothing to hide.

It's okay to make the wholehearted process my own.

When I forgive, I feel less burdened and more free.

Part 3

GROW

Whilst researching this book, I was keen to understand the internal struggles that impede people's confidence and the practices that help them to feel more empowered, compassionate and accepting of themselves. So, I read over thousands of comments in my online classroom. Whilst many of these comments related to people's experiences, there were also entries about people's opinions of the course and of me.

Whilst reading over these comments, an interesting (but not surprising) thing happened. I became desensitised to the positive comments and hyper-alert to the negative ones.

When I was learning about people's heartwarming breakthroughs (the moments they forgave themselves, healed childhood wounds, set clear boundaries or embarked on brave adventures), I wasn't totally present or relaxed. Rather than sinking into the fullness of these moments, I could feel my physical body bracing for the possibility of the next negative comment (of which I might add, there were only a few).

Despite all our scientific and technological breakthroughs and my decade-long meditation practice, at that moment, I was just like our ancestors from thousands of years ago - cooking by the fire, unable to totally relax and enjoy the bounty of the day, on the lookout for the sabre-toothed tiger in the distance.

Our human tendency to focus more on 'threats' than 'opportunities' is referred to as our inbuilt 'negativity bias'. Whilst this bias is important for our survival, if left unexamined it can negatively skew the way we see the world and our place in it.

So, what is the science behind this negativity bias? Neuroscientist Dr Rick Hanson explains that our brains have specialised circuits that register negative experiences immediately into our emotional memory. Put simply, negative memories (and the associated emotions) stick. In contrast, positive experiences have standard-issue memory systems. Unless we really focus on them, they don't transfer from short-term memory into long-term storage. In other words, they don't stick.

Take a minute now to think about how this negativity bias plays out for you. Do you:

- lie in bed at night and focus on that one silly comment you made in a work meeting, rather than on all the ways you added value to the conversation?

- criticise yourself for having one unhealthy meal or a day without exercise whilst rarely taking a moment to acknowledge all the times you eat well and move your body?

- ruminate about the time you raised your voice with your children whilst failing to acknowledge all the moments you were calm and patient?

Walking the wholehearted confidence path includes acknowledging your negativity bias and taking time each day to intentionally shift your awareness away from perceived threats towards opportunities. Neuroscientists and meditation teachers often refer to this practice of reorienting as 'growing the good'. The key feature of this practice is lingering in the positive experience for at least a few minutes.

STEP ONE: NOTICE THE GOOD.

If your child offers you a hug, if your partner makes you a cup of coffee, if you observe the first flowers of spring, pause and really notice the moment.

STEP TWO: GROW THE GOOD.

Expand the moment by engaging your senses. Breathe deeply. Notice any feelings of relaxation or aliveness in your body. Feel this moment in your heart, not just your mind. Trust that as you linger in this moment for a few minutes you are moving the experience from short to long-term memory in your brain.

There are thousands of ways the negativity bias can play out. What we perceive as threats will depend on our upbringing, the culture and political context we live in, our values, beliefs and so on. What we see as threats may also change over time as we age, our responsibilities change and our external world transforms.

For example, when you are a teenager, not having the same clothes as your friends or the latest iPhone may feel like a threat (to your social safety). When you are middle-aged with children, the threat of losing

Linger in the good times
long enough

for them to land
in your mind
body
and
heart

your job may feel heightened as you fear not being able to pay the mortgage or the school fees. As you age, health concerns and the threat of disease may consume your awareness.

So, how can you begin to understand your unique negativity bias? How can you become more skilled at identifying the ways you get hooked? We can begin by understanding our basic human needs and the different ways these may feel threatened.

In their book, *Resilient*, Dr Hanson and his son Forrest share that humans have three fundamental needs: safety, satisfaction and connection. We can use these as a framework for understanding threats and moving towards opportunities.

Read over the examples below and notice which ones you can relate to most strongly. Do you focus most on the threat to safety, satisfaction or connection? Or does your negativity bias include a combination?

THREAT TO SAFETY

- Hearing that a friend's car or house was broken into and then worrying that someone is going to break into your car or house at night, hurt the kids or steal your valuables.
- Googling a health concern and then spiralling into anxiety or worst-case scenario.
- Reading about a natural disaster on the other side of the world and then thinking that the bad weather in your neighbourhood might turn into something more sinister.

- Planning a holiday, but also worrying that the food, accommodation or weather may be disappointing.
- Focusing on the repetitive or mundane nature of your job and not on how you are making a difference in people's lives through your work.
- Hearing about someone's promotion, new relationship or home and feeling like your life isn't rewarding.

THREAT TO CONNECTION

- Ruminating about all the ways your partner/children don't appreciate you.
- Worrying that you have said or done something to disappoint a friend.
- Feeling like you have let the team down at work.

Have you ever noticed that you can handle some types of criticism better than other types or that what feels like a threat to you, doesn't for others? Maybe at work you don't feel threatened when your boss offers some suggestions for improving a project you are working on, but when a friend hints that you have let them down, it brings up all sorts of uncomfortable emotions and makes you question who you are.

Perhaps you have noticed that when you and your partner are planning a weekend away, you focus more on all the things that could go wrong whilst your partner just packs a bag and trusts that it will all work out.

This 'not all perceived threats are equal' possibility played out for me whilst reading through all the comments in my online classroom.

The first three negative comments were: *Her voice is slow and annoying, She sounds like a robot*, and, *Why doesn't she pronounce her Rs properly?* To which I responded (in my mind), *Well, my voice is my voice, I can't do much about it so I'm not going to let those comments worry me.*

From a neuroscience perspective, my response didn't contain a negative emotional charge significant enough for it to land in my long-term memory. And, in case you were wondering about why I don't pronounce my Rs properly, Australian speech is non-rhotic, we don't pronounce the Rs at the end of words. Every now and then this really annoys someone!

The next comment, however, cut deep. This person expressed their displeasure with me 'sharing my eco-social views' in my meditation course. I can't be certain, but I imagine they were referring to me mentioning that profits from the course were going towards providing malaria nets to children with disabilities in Africa, and that I believed we can use meditation not only to improve our own lives but also as a tool for positive social change.

When I read that comment, I felt my posture shift. My shoulders turned inwards (as a way to protect my heart). I felt an uncomfortable combination of shame and vulnerability. And you guessed it, with such a strong emotional charge, my brain stored this experience in my long-term memory, hence why even now as I write this, I feel uncomfortable.

So, why was it easy for me to brush off the first set of 'negative' comments, but not the second? The latter awakened shadows deep within me, exposing some of my oldest conditioned beliefs. Shadows that whisper, *You're not safe to express your true feelings, if you make other people feel uncomfortable, they won't love or accept you.*

It doesn't matter how much almond milk we drink, how many times we have chanted 'Om' on the yoga mat or the amount of money we have invested in therapy or self-help books, our negativity bias is part of being human.

Wholehearted confidence isn't about eradicating our negativity bias, it's about getting to know the ways we are pulled in by these perceived threats. It's an invitation to stay curious, make connections to our shadows and carve out time to reorient our awareness towards opportunities to feel safe, satisfied and connected. And remember, you need to linger in these opportunities so that they really land. Let's explore opportunities and ways to 'grow the good' together now.

OPPORTUNITIES FOR SAFETY

- When you are home at night, take the time to notice all the elements in your home that make you feel safe. For example, the locked door, the roof, heating or cooling, food in your fridge and so on. Take a few deep breaths into this feeling of safety.

- Take a moment to scan your body and feel grateful for all the ways it supports you each day. Your heart beats, your lungs breathe, you digest food, walk, talk, see, hear etc. Whisper to yourself: *Thank you, body, for supporting me all day, every day.*

- Look out for examples of feeling at home in your neighbourhood. Is there a park you enjoy? Does your dog love to sniff around the streets? Do your local shops have fresh produce or a great place to get coffee? Take in these small pleasures in your community.

OPPORTUNITIES FOR SATISFACTION

- Take some time to reflect on all the ways you help people, either directly or directly - at home, with friends, at work. Allow this sense of satisfaction to relax your body.

- Think back to the last time you had fun or experienced great pleasure. Really bring the details to mind. Allow this memory to land in your body, mind and heart.

- Savour a meal. Eat mindfully. Put your phone down. Notice the different colours, textures and flavours. Really feel into this experience of satisfaction.

- Make a commitment to put your phone down when friends, family or colleagues speak to you. Listen mindfully. Notice facial expressions, the emotions sitting underneath the words and their desire to feel seen and heard.

- Look for small signs that people appreciate you. Notice when people pay you a compliment, express their gratitude or just say thank you. Take a few deep breaths into these moments and feel them in your body.

- Take a walk and connect with nature and the season you are in. Notice the colours, textures and signs of life. Reflect on an aspect of your life that aligns with the natural season you are in.

Think about your own life right now. What perceived threat have you been focusing on? How could you grow the good in this situation?

Now see if you can make a positive statement in relation to moving away from threat towards opportunity. For example: *When I notice myself worrying about whether my colleagues like me or not, I will intentionally shift my focus towards examples of how I am valued by friends and family.*

I remind myself that I am safe

I linger in moments
of satisfaction

I notice signs that
I belong

Given that wholehearted confidence is also about improving our relationships with others, let's use what we have learnt about the negativity bias and the importance of shifting from threats to opportunities to both understand and improve our relationships.

As Pema Chodron reflects in her book, *When Things Fall Apart*:

> 'When we become more insightful and compassionate about the ways we get hooked, we spontaneously feel tenderness for the human race. Knowing our own confusion, we're more willing and able to get our hands dirty and try to alleviate the confusion of others.'

So together, let's get curious about the experience of someone we care about.

MINDFUL PRACTICE INSIDE THE MIND OF ANOTHER

Understanding our own mind allows a window into the minds of family, friends, colleagues and even strangers. So, begin by taking a few deep breaths in the wholehearted posture. Sky. Body. Earth.

Once you feel settled and receptive, think of someone who you would like to understand more, or feel closer to. With curiosity, reflect on these questions:

- Do they see the world through the lens of safety? Do they often worry about their physical health, the demise of their community or the state of the world?

- Is feeling satisfied at work, with friends, food or fun important to them? Do they wonder about their purpose or worry that their life isn't exciting, interesting or satisfying enough?

- Are relationships important to them? Do they fear letting others down? Do they place pressure on themselves to get things right? Do they often feel like they are doing so much for others but aren't being appreciated?

Take a few deep breaths. Reconnect with the wholehearted posture. As your heart opens, connect to our shared human needs.

Ask yourself: *How could I support this person to feel more safe, satisfied or connected?*

Transform this reflection into a positive statement. For example: *When I notice this person focusing on how boring or routine-driven life feels for them, I will suggest something fun and pleasurable to do together.*

Well done, you've just used your wholehearted confidence to both understand and support someone else!

WHY GROWING THE GOOD
CAN FEEL HARD

Now that we have walked through the process of understanding our basic human needs and shifting our awareness from perceived threats to opportunities, you might be wondering, *Why don't we do this all the time?* Why aren't we all walking through life feeling safe in our bodies and our homes, satisfied at work and in life, and connected to family and friends in honest and rewarding ways?

Well, the first and most obvious reason is that there are real threats in life. Someone could break into our car, you might lose your job, your relationships may end. But the truth is, we often exaggerate these threats in our minds and spend a disproportionate amount of time focusing on them.

The second reason is that our negativity bias has a very loyal and committed friend - the ego. That little voice inside your head that tells you something bad will happen if you relax and let your guard down, that's it's not safe to rest when you are tired. The inner critic who says on repeat that you aren't enough or that you are too much. The fear that tricks you into thinking your family will be disappointed if you don't attend to their needs over your own.

There are many different psychological and spiritual interpretations of the ego. For the purpose of this book, let's view the ego as the internal voice that spoils things, puts us down and tries desperately to make us feel separate and not enough. The ego creeps into our shadows, our negativity bias and our humanity.

If you are keen to understand how your ego presents itself, think about the most repetitive, familiar, heavy or cautionary things you say to yourself or worry about. This is your ego! Oh, so boring but oh, so captivating!

The ego is designed to keep us small, afraid and disconnected from our deeper nature. When we are caught in its energy we may:

- feel nervous about sharing our ideas in work meetings.
- reject invitations to do things socially.
- avoid stepping out of our comfort zone and trying new things.
- resist sharing our true feelings with our partner or friends.
- ignore our body's signs that we are tired.

When we attempt to reorient our awareness away from threat towards opportunity, it's common for our ego to get loud. In my community, the ego's resistance wore many disguises. It expressed itself as anger and frustration. ('This activity is stupid, what's the point anyway?') It showed itself as a feeling of numbness.

Participants shared how they 'stared at a blank canvas' when asked to think of some examples of their basic goodness. The ego also dressed up as confusion. One participant said, 'It felt like standing in front of a locked door rifling through a large set of keys looking for the right one to fit.'

So, how can you move past the ego towards your inherent goodness and your inner dimensions that feel safe, satisfied and connected? You can begin by following these four steps.

1. **Get to know your ego.** Get curious about the words it says to you. Notice when it is most persistent. Remember, think about the most repetitive and boring stories you tell yourself, and this is your ego!

2. **Normalise the resistance.** Acknowledge that your ego will get loud when you begin the process of reorienting your awareness. See the pushback as a natural part of the process rather than as a sign that there aren't opportunities for safety, satisfaction or connection. For example, if you draw a blank when trying to think of reasons why people would appreciate you, that's not because there is nothing to appreciate within you, it's because your ego is very sneaky and persuasive.

3. **Be firm.** Say to your ego, *Not now*, in a calm but strict way. (You will notice this is a different approach to befriending our shadows as we explored in part two.)

4. **Meditate.** The practice of meditation allows us to shift our focus from the level of the ego and instinct (the work of the limbic system and the amygdala) towards our deeper nature. From here, it feels easier to identify opportunities for safety, satisfaction and connection and to let these land through the practice of meditation.

In meditation
we move from ego
and instinct

towards our
deeper nature

Just as we were able to use our understanding of the negativity bias to feel closer to others, we can also strengthen our relationships through awareness of the ego.

After working with people all around the world, I've noticed that often, our egos are all telling us the same story - that there is something wrong with us. Maybe yours tells you that you are too much whilst mine tells me I'm not enough. Either way, the message is the same - it's not safe to accept yourself as you are.

Sometimes I like to imagine that there is one giant ego operating in the sky - an energetic force that we all tap into. For me, this idea that a collective ego lives 'out there' rather than 'inside me' helps create space. From here, I am able to unhook.

Understanding the more collective nature of the ego also helps me to feel closer to other humans - family, friends, even strangers. I imagine us all walking around plugged into this giant shared ego in the sky. From here, I feel greater compassion and understanding for the human condition.

How do you feel about the possibility of one giant collective ego that we all tap into? Can you use this image to help you take your own ego less personally? Can it create space for greater compassion and understanding?

I remember when I first started teaching mindfulness and meditation about nine years ago. It was my career reinvention after having kids. I was keen to do a great job and determined to help people break free from the habits that kept them tired, stressed and self-critical.

I spent hours preparing for the classes. I created beautiful and comprehensive workbooks. I used my decade-long experience in education to design courses that took people on a journey and allowed ideas and experiences to progress naturally. I kept the groups small so that people felt safe to share. I even gave people little gifts!

Looking back on that time, I can see that, whilst some of these actions were driven by my wholesome desire to help people, my ego was exerting itself too. It was whispering to me, *Your classes need to be perfect*, and, *It's your responsibility to convince people to be more mindful so that they can be truly happy (and think you are amazing in the process!)*.

It didn't matter how prepared I was, how thorough my workbooks were or how many blankets or pillows I provided so people could feel comfortable, some participants just weren't able to embrace the ideas or the opportunities presented. Their egos were putting up a fight, resisting in all sorts of ways. They were saying things like, 'I don't have time to meditate,' and, 'I could never take time for self-care when there are dishes in the sink and washing to do.'

And of course, my ego responded by taking their resistance personally. It said to me, *You didn't do enough, it's your fault they weren't able to develop a meditation practice or be kind to themselves*.

Learning about my own ego and the shared ego helped me to see that the experience of my students had nothing to do with me. What a relief! Knowing that I wasn't responsible for convincing other people's egos of anything was life-changing for me both professionally and personally.

At work, I let go of the impossible and exhausting task of trying to control people's experiences and instead, leaned into teaching with more presence, creativity and trust.

Personally, this awareness of the ego has allowed me to feel less responsible for my family's happiness and more able to support my children to solve their own problems rather than jumping in with solutions. In short, I realised that I wasn't the main character in every situation. I learned to take life less personally.

When we hold strong to the idea that not everything is about us (sorry, ego!), we feel less knocked about by our external world and more grounded and confident.

How can this experience of mine help you to see your relationships more clearly? Perhaps there is someone in your life who you feel overly responsible for. Maybe, when your kids are unhappy, you think it's because you have done something wrong or that it's your job to make it better. Or have you been trying to convince someone to change, to develop healthy eating habits, to drink less, do more exercise or meditate?

Can you see how both your egos are interacting within these dynamics?

So far, we have explored getting to know our negativity bias, saying *not now* to our ego, normalising resistance and letting opportunities for safety, satisfaction and connection land. Another practice that can deepen this experience and help us feel more wholeheartedly confident is learning to cultivate our discerning nature - the ability to see reality for what it is.

Whilst the practice of discernment has religious roots, it can also be explored in a secular way. When we weave it together with mindfulness and meditation, the result is often an ability to see ourselves, our habits and actions more clearly.

As mindfulness and meditation expert Sharon Salzberg reflects, 'Increased awareness enables us to discern whether a particular experience we are having is one that we want to put more energy into, or one that we want to stand back from and allow to fade away.'

It can, for example, help us decide if we want to maintain or let go of certain friendships. It can support us when trying to establish healthy habits. We can use it at work when deciding whether to speak up or move on.

Discernment in the context of wholehearted confidence is also about taking aligned action from this grounded place of awareness. Through feeling into what we need and don't need, by connecting with our deeper nature to discover what's working and what's not, we can approach decision-making and our daily lives from a more aligned position.

This sense of embodiment between desire and action helps to conquer the divide many of us experience between knowing we should do something ... and actually doing it!

As one community member commented:

'It's interesting and frustrating to me that, while I clearly know which actions are fundamental to my contentment (or discontentment) in life, there seems to be a consistent disconnect within me between knowing and doing (or not doing). It really helps to realise that discernment is a practice I can strengthen. Knowing I always have a choice in how I want to live my life. Perhaps that choice, that trust in my sovereignty, that deciding, is precisely the connection between the knowing and the doing. Discernment could be the key to freedom!'

MINDFUL PRACTICE
LET YOUR BREATH BE
YOUR GUIDE

So how can you begin to cultivate your discerning nature? The simplest way is to use your breath with this two-step practice.

STEP ONE: FOCUS ON YOUR INHALE.

Notice how when you breathe in, your whole body expands and you take up more space. Ask yourself: *What do I want to expand into?*

STEP TWO: FOCUS ON YOUR EXHALE.

Notice how when you breathe out, your whole body contracts and you take up less space. Ask yourself: *What do I want to move away from?*

When people in my community used their breath and meditation to practise discernment, it became clear what they wanted to move away from and what they wanted to move closer towards. Here is what they said:

Unhealthy food habits

'I desire to move away from mindless snacking by pausing and getting curious about what I really need in these moments. I will shift my attention towards fulfilling this need in another way.'

Negative self-talk

'I commit to moving away from negative self-talk by pausing and asking myself if these statements are true or if they are just stories. If they are stories, I'll use my discerning nature to create new, more supportive and courageous narratives.'

Pleasing others

'I am ready to move away from my habit of doing what suits everyone else. When I notice the resentment creeping in, I'll get curious and enquire about what I really want and how I can get closer to that.'

Social media

'When I spend too much time on social media, I'll get curious and ask myself, *What am I yearning for here?* I will try and give myself this in another way.'

Gossip

'When I notice myself talking negatively about work with colleagues, I will change the subject, share something I am grateful for or an aspect of my job that I enjoy.'

Accepting change

'I am ready to stop resisting the changes at work. Moving forward, I will pause and try to be more accepting of the new structures and systems that have been recently implemented.'

Long hours at the computer

'When I observe my body getting tight or sore after being at the computer, I will take a break, do a few stretches or enjoy a walk around the block.'

Over-giving

'I am ready to create healthy boundaries.'

Being distracted

'When I notice that I am on my phone when the kids are wanting to engage with me, I will put my phone away and lean into being present with them.'

Judging family and friends

'It's time to soften the judgement I make about family and friends, and instead, remind myself that we are all trying our best.'

Rest

'I am ready to stop pushing through when I am tired, and instead, allowing myself to rest, meditate and spend time in nature when I am feeling tired and depleted.'

Did you resonate with any of these comments? What would you like to move away from? What do you yearn to move towards? Try this practice to delve deeper into your discerning nature.

VISUALISATION PRACTICE
QUIET TIME IN THE CEMETERY

Find a comfortable place to sit. Focus your awareness on the space between your two eyebrows. Send a feeling of calm there. Trust that as you focus on this space (your prefrontal cortex), you are softening your limbic system, amygdala and your ego. This will help you feel less emotionally charged and more able to see things clearly.

Imagine that you are taking a walk in a cemetery. You notice the grass underfoot, the tiny wildflowers and weeds. You place your hand on a tombstone and feel its cool, rough texture beneath your fingertips. You scan a few names and dates. You wonder what their lives were like, the joys and challenges they lived through. Being here offers you the gift of perspective and clarity. Everyone here is dead, but you are alive.

You find a patch of grass in the sun, and you sit down. You allow your awareness to rest on your breath. You notice how, when you breathe in, your whole body expands, and you take up more space. With every exhale, your whole body contracts and you take up less space.

Here in the stillness of the graveyard, you reflect on the following four questions:

1. If I truly believed in my discerning nature, what habits or activities would I let go?
2. What conversations, stories or situations would I no longer get hooked into?
3. If I truly believed my time was precious and to be valued, what would I do more of?
4. What would I no longer put off?

And for your final few moments at the cemetery, imagine yourself acting in this way over the coming days. Really picture it in your mind. Trust that, as you do, you are letting this moment of discernment land.

THE SAFETY SCAVENGER HUNT

We watch the news and receive an image of the world that is both frightening and disheartening. The world is presented to us twenty-four seven as a planet in crisis, where horrendous crimes, political corruption and endless conflict are the norm. We receive a call from our children's school, our body tenses up, we brace ourselves for the news of a broken arm or split lip. We hear a car alarm go off and a wave of heat moves through our body. The dog barks late at night and we check that the front door is locked.

It feels like we are surrounded by threats, stresses and challenges, but what are we missing?

During this time, our partner makes us a cup of tea. Flowers bloom in the local park. Foreign aid gets sent to a war-torn country. Your children walk the dog. An old friend calls to see how you are.

But given our negativity bias, unless we make an effort to register these small clues that we are safe, these moments go by largely unnoticed.

Add a layer of persistent low-level stress caused by the demands of our over-scheduled lives (and the residue from the pandemic) and the threats feel magnified whilst our capacity to gain perspective, regulate our emotions and creatively problem-solve are diminished.

So, how can we begin to break free from this sense of hypervigilance, our natural tendency to think or imagine the worst? The first step is to notice what happens in your body when your awareness is focused on threats to safety.

- Do your shoulders creep up around your ears?
- Do you get a tight feeling in your gut?
- Do you clench your jaw, grind your teeth or hold your breath?

Becoming familiar with the way your body carries stress and this habitual sense of anticipation is helpful. From here we can get intentional about softening these physical manifestations. When we relax physically, our nervous system feels safe, and we can feel safe in the world.

Having lived for many years with a chronic pain condition that resulted in a nearly permanent state of fight or flight, I've tried many different practices for soothing my nervous system. Of course, there's meditation, mindfulness, yoga, tai chi and so on. Joining a choir, taking an art class or learning an instrument might even help.

But there's one simple practice that stands out for me in terms of ease and impact. I call it the 'safety scavenger hunt'. You don't need to enrol in a class or wear a special outfit. All you need to do is move through your day with the intention of identifying ten things that offer you a feeling of safety - physical, psychological, emotional or spiritual.

Here's a list of what I noticed in my community yesterday.

1. A neighbour put a water bowl out for the local dogs.
2. A man let me out in traffic.
3. My chiropractor gave me a hug.
4. The autumn sun shone through my front window.
5. My husband scrubbed the pot I burnt.
6. My youngest son told me I looked pretty in my new dress.
7. The local government implemented a new compost system for food scraps.
8. The bus driver waved at me.
9. A new store opened that sells packaging-free products.
10. The street sweeper collected all the autumn leaves.

You can keep a running tally of things in your head, write them in your journal or in the notes section of your phone. See how your list grows over a day, a week or a month. Read over the list and allow all these small signs of safety to land. I wonder just how much safety you could notice in your community if you set your mind to it?

My eldest son is fourteen years old and over six feet tall. He loves food. It's a key ingredient in his level of satisfaction, excuse the pun. 'Mum, what's for dinner?' he asks as he walks in the door from school. Maybe you also have a child who enjoys food. Perhaps you know someone who loves to go out for dinner, reading the reviews and menus beforehand, giving themselves the best possible chance of avoiding the threat of a disappointing meal.

Obviously, satisfaction doesn't only relate to food. We can experience this sense of being full, of there being enough, in relation to our home, work, relationships or the activities we enjoy.

Perhaps for you it's important to feel purposeful at work. Maybe you like to give back to your community as a way to feel satisfied. Or is having fun, going on adventures or catching up with friends what gives you pleasure and allows you to feel whole?

LOOK INWARDS

It's natural to seek satisfaction from our external world, through praise from our boss, recognition at home or validation from friends. Many of us have been seeking (consciously or subconsciously) this external validation for a lifetime, telling ourselves that when we finally receive the recognition we deserve, then we'll feel confident.

Wholehearted confidence challenges this script by gently inviting us inwards to our own sense of inherent goodness. This doesn't mean that we are perfect, always noble or never make an error in judgement. Rather, it includes a willingness to connect with our good intentions, wise actions and ability to show up, time and time again, for this one precious life and those we care about.

When we can cultivate a connection with this aspect of ourselves, we feel less thrown about by challenges, more able to walk steadily on shaky ground and to support family, friends, colleagues and our community.

So, after years of focusing on your flaws, believing that being hard on yourself is a good motivator and waiting for others to assure you of your worth, it can feel challenging to shift your awareness towards your inherent goodness.

Where do you begin? A great place to start is to create an inventory of some recent examples of when your actions revealed your basic goodness. Interestingly, people in my community found it easiest to identify wholesome aspects of themselves as they related to their values. So, let's do this together now.

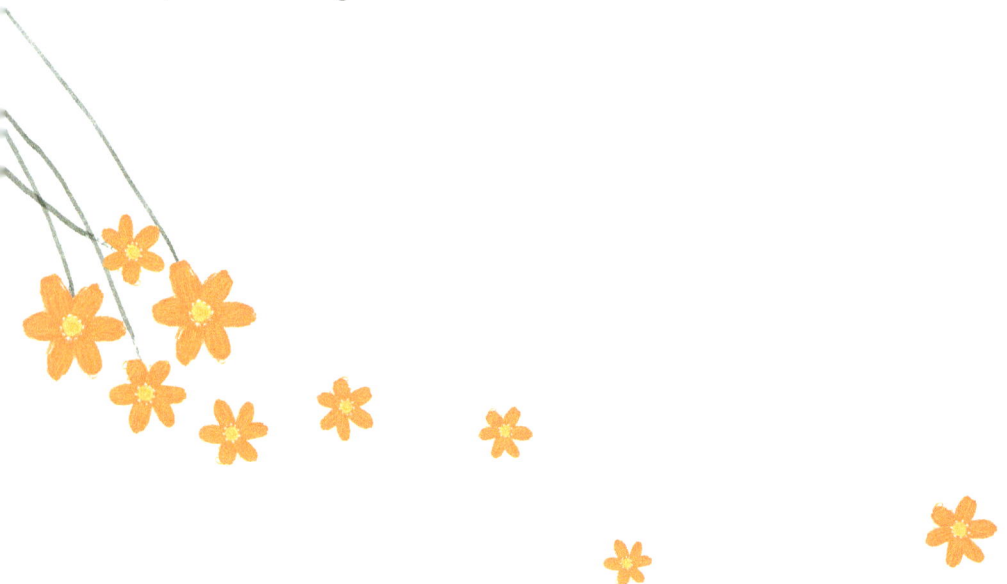

WRITING PRACTICE
USE YOUR VALUES
AS AN ANCHOR

Settle into the wholehearted posture. Imagine that the sky is smiling at you. Take a few deep breaths. Send this smile into your body and then into the earth beneath you. Imagine that the earth holds the memories of all the times you have made good decisions, acted from your values, supported family, friends and colleagues.

Focus for a moment on the space between your two eyebrows. Picture an ice block melting in the sun. Trust that this awareness is engaging your prefrontal cortex and quietening your limbic system so that you can see yourself and your deeper nature more clearly.

Turn to the values list in part one on page 53. Remember that there are no good or bad values. Pick four and write them down. Now think about how you have lived these values recently. Write down two examples for each value – that's eight in total.

For example, if you chose the value of connection, you might think about a time recently when you really listened to a friend, spent time in nature or in meditation.

Remember that these acts don't need to be out of the ordinary.

Read over the list with a willingness to feel into your own inherent goodness. If the little voice in your head starts saying things like, *These acts aren't special, they are just a normal part of life, everyone does them*, take a breath. Place your hand on your heart and relax your body.

Repeat silently in your mind a few times: *I am safe to acknowledge the goodness that lives within me.*

CONFIDENCE IN ACTION - MAKING & LOSING FRIENDS

Chris grew up in a volatile environment. Her father was an alcoholic and violent towards her and her mother. When the violence escalated, she was forced to stay with neighbours who were well-meaning, but also strangely curious about the private details of her domestic life.

Chris closed off from the world. As an adult, she only let two people in - her husband and her best friend, Maddy.

Chris reflected on the beginning of their friendship. She shared, 'I'm not a social being. I'm stand-offish, shy and move away from anyone who tries to get to know me. That was before I met her. She was determined that we would be best friends. She asked me one day if I liked to bike ride. I said yes and felt I would be comfortable doing this with her. A jaunt around the block, what harm. Little did I know she was planning a century bike ride, that's one hundred miles! Maddy was warm, kind and the nicest person I had ever met.'

Not too long after they became best friends, Maddy received a cancer diagnosis. Sitting in the doctor's room hearing that her best friend was so ill, Chris' first thought was, *I have finally let someone in and now ...* Her next thought was, *Don't cry, Maddy needs me to be strong.*

Ever since she was young, Chris had been strong and able to handle the 'ugly' parts of her life without assistance. This time felt different. Aware that she needed help, Chris reached out to the mental health department. She broke down in tears at the appointment. The experience in the doctor's room and also at the mental health department made her feel ashamed and weak.

Amidst the tears, she apologised for being out of control, to which the counsellor responded, 'I don't see a person who is out of control. I see a person who loves her friend so much that she came here to deal with her grief so she could help her friend with hers.'

Chris' best friend died ten months later. Chris reflected, 'During that time, we cried, we laughed at past antics, we raged in disgust about this horrible disease. Our display of emotions defined what an incredible loving bond our friendship had. Maddy died peacefully knowing that her best friend loved her and had shown her how much she would be missed.'

We can all seek inspiration from Chris' story. By breaking the habit of going it alone and instead, asking for help, she reminds us of the power of letting people in. By allowing her courage to be peppered with vulnerability, Chris encourages us to expand our own understanding of what it looks and feels like to be brave.

Finally, by accepting her entire experience without judgement (including the feelings of shame and fear) she was able to support Maddy through her experience too. This is a powerful reminder that our own growth has a positive ripple in the lives of others.

MEETING OUR NEED FOR CONNECTION

No doubt you've heard the phrase 'humans are wired for connection' or 'loneliness is worse than smoking'. These catchcries point to our deep need to feel loved, liked and appreciated for who we are (not who we strive or pretend to be).

For our ancestors, feeling connected had a self-preservation aspect to it. If we were valued by others, they would want to keep us around, so we would be safe from threats in the comfort of our tribe.

But we all know that in our modern world, relationships are complicated. Stress, time pressures, competing demands, inflated egos, unmet expectations and lingering hurts all stand between us and a deep experience of feeling seen and heard.

That's why taking the time to explore the different ways you are valued by family, friends, colleagues (even acquaintances or strangers) is a powerful way to have our need for connection met. From here, we can feel more confident in ourselves and our place in the world.

FEELING VALUED AGAINST THE ODDS

Our relationships often carry the strain of our over-scheduled lives. After a busy day at work, we cook dinner and the kids move the food around the plate with disinterest, unaware of the effort it took to prepare.

We try to tell our partner how we are feeling, and they nod but don't look up from their phone. We respond to work emails on the weekend, but our boss rarely acknowledges the extra hours. We go for a walk and listen to our friend talk about her unhappy marriage even when we are exhausted and in need of rest.

Over time, these discrete moments add up. We feel unappreciated and unvalued. We internalise this experience. Then, we look out for more evidence that people don't appreciate our efforts. Our kids or partner leave their wet towel on the bathroom floor and our ego squeals in delight! It says, *See, I told you no-one appreciates you!*

Part of the wholehearted confidence process is taking the time to focus on the ways we are valued by others so that we can break this unhealthy cycle.

The good news is that you don't need to wait for someone to thank you for your efforts or express their gratitude. You can begin right now by taking a few minutes to pause and reflect on these questions:

- Do your friends or family value your good intentions, the way you genuinely want to help others, to do the right thing or make people feel comfortable?
- Do they value your good character, whether you are honest, loyal or reliable?
- Do they appreciate what's in your heart, your compassion, the way you feel joy or gratitude?

Perhaps over the years people have admired your skills, either innate or learnt. Are you musical, creative, coordinated or good with animals? Do you have skills related to your work that colleagues might admire? Or is it the choices you have made in life, the way you have bounced back from adversity or taken risks that people really notice and admire?

Still feeling unsure? Read over the following list and pick two or three ways people might value you.

Character
Are you loyal, reliable, honest, consistent, lighthearted, gentle, balanced, forgiving?

Personality
Are you funny, creative, musical, curious, even-tempered, weird?

Intentions
Do you desire to: help people feel comfortable, be authentic, do what you say you will, listen, care for others, live a meaningful life?

Heart

Do you share your love, gratitude, compassion, hope, joy, insight, wisdom or perspective with others?

Skills

Can you cook, dance, sing, draw, garden, build, fix? Do you have specific work-related abilities?

Choices

Have you bounced back from adversity, made brave career choices, moved across the country, travelled, studied later in life, ended unhealthy relationships, healed from trauma, broken unhealthy family patterns, committed to being present and happy?

As you can see from the above list, there are so many (and more) ways that people can value and appreciate you. That's why it's so interesting to note that, even when offered all these different suggestions, people in my community still found this practice difficult.

Perhaps, like some of the participants in my research, you grew up in a family where valuing your skills or talents meant you were vain or arrogant? Or does your cultural background encourage you to put your head down and not draw attention to yourself, your skills or gifts?

Or maybe the whole experience just feels uncomfortable, challenging habits of a lifetime or tapping into some inner vulnerability. As part of the wholehearted journey, George explored all the *clever* ways his ego pushed back on the opportunity to feel appreciated by others. Perhaps you can relate?

APPRECIATE the
APPRECIATION

You might remember George, the man who experienced imposter syndrome at work but not as a budding poet! During the process of reorienting, George was able to identify signs that he was valued.

He acknowledged that his wife took care of him when he was sick. His friend sent him a nice voice message. His manager gave him some positive feedback. But what emerged more powerfully for George was how strong his resistance was to receiving the gift of being valued.

George noticed how, when people paid him a compliment, his immediate reaction was to deflect or negate. He would minimise these moments by saying 'oh, it's nothing' or 'I should have done it sooner'. Sometimes, he even directed the credit to others, commenting 'it wasn't all me, the team helped a lot'.

George also noticed how he would rush to reciprocate the compliment. This not only detracted from the moment, but also felt stressful as he had to come up with some positive words in an instant. It felt forced, not natural.

George is learning to appreciate the appreciation. His new response is, 'you're welcome'.

Perhaps you have your own funny little ways of pushing back on the compliments or the appreciation expressed by others. Do you avoid eye contact? Do you make a joke or change the subject? I hope you'll explore how to appreciate the appreciation in the following practice.

MINDFUL PRACTICE
BEYOND THE RESISTANCE

Focus on the point between your eyebrows. Hold the image of an ice block melting in the sun in your mind's eye.

Imagine that as you focus on your prefrontal cortex, you are relaxing the limbic brain and softening the emotional charge associated with feeling unappreciated.

Now think of someone you love or like. Imagine that this person is smiling at you. Take a few deep breaths. Notice any sense of relaxation in your body as you feel their smile.

Ask yourself: *What are some of the ways this person values me?* (Refer to the previous list on page 174 if needed.)

Now, imagine this person paying you a compliment, or expressing their appreciation. Notice any desire to resist the compliment. If your ego gets loud, respond clearly and firmly with the statement not now.

Imagine yourself accepting this gesture of appreciation like a gift, with presence and gratitude. What words would you say? How would it feel in your body and in your heart?

Stay in this feeling of being appreciated for five breaths. Let the moment land. Trust that you are transferring this experience of being valued into your long-term memory.

Well done! You just created an opportunity where your need for connection was met, helping you to feel more wholeheartedly confident.

When we allow ourselves to identify and *feel* how others value us, it acts like a mirror revealing our wholesomeness. We can internalise this feeling so that we value ourselves. And from here, we are more likely to value others. So, this positive cycle of feeling valued, valuing ourselves and then valuing others continues, each aspect strengthening our sense of confidence and connection.

Together, let's create this positive cycle by reflecting on these questions:

- After exploring the previous activity, what is one thing you can value about yourself? Feel this as more than a thought. Allow it to land in your body.

- Think about the person from the previous activity and identify three things you value about them. Feel this sense of valuing in your body. Linger in this moment and in this opportunity for connection.

GROW

Ava was born in New Zealand and is currently living in Japan. She is the co-founder of a charity supporting communities to break the cycle of poverty. Through my own social enterprise, *The Happy Habit*, I support her charity and I have seen, on more than one occasion, how she downplays the incredible work she does.

That's why it was such a pleasure for me to hear about her latest trip to the school she supports in Indonesia.

'The minute I stepped into the preschool in Indonesia where the kids were singing, I was overwhelmed by the joy in them,' said Ava. 'I was so moved by the opportunity their school gave them to live a life free of poverty (something they probably don't understand yet at their young age), but it was like the room was full of the hope and potential that the charity preschool provided. It was an incredible feeling.'

When Ava's eyes met with one of the teachers whose salary she had fundraised for, they both crossed the room and hugged each other tightly with tears in their eyes. 'She was so grateful to me for fundraising for her salary and the school, and I was so grateful to her for giving a loving, quality education to these kids who deserved so much,' commented Ava.

'She handed me a card she'd made that said, *Thank you for supporting me, from the bottom of my heart.* I've received things like this in the past and thought they were nice, but this one really landed for me. I felt deeply that my work was making a difference for people and that my efforts were appreciated by them.'

Ava's experience highlights how when we open our hearts to appreciation, life feels bigger, brighter and more beautiful. Sensing the joy in the room, feeling the contribution she was making, receiving and expressing gratitude - all these moments were felt more deeply.

PART THREE: SELF-REFLECTION

After getting to know your negativity bias and your ego, and using these insights to strengthen your relationships, ability to see things clearly and feel safe, satisfied and connected, take some time to reflect on these questions:

1. Do you feel most inspired to move from threat to opportunity in relation to your core need for safety, satisfaction or connection?

2. What will you say to your ego when it tries to keep you small, afraid, separate or not enough?

3. When might you use the breath of discernment to help you make decisions or guide your actions?

YOUR
CONFIDENCE
COMMITMENTS

Repeat these phrases in the morning or at night either out loud or in your mind. Write them in your journal or on a Post-it Note. Use them anytime you want to drop into the feeling of wholehearted confidence.

I pause and reorient my awareness towards more positive aspects of myself and my life.

I notice when my ego is loud, and I take the necessary steps to feel less hooked in.

When making decisions, I connect to my breath and my discerning nature.

I remind myself that I am safe.

I linger in moments of satisfaction.

I notice signs (both big and small) that I belong.

Part 4

EXPAND

Over the years, I've had many light-bulb moments that have allowed me to understand myself more deeply, feel less anxious, more empowered and confident. The most illuminating discovery has been learning that our physical body speaks to us all day every day and that, if we don't listen to its whispers, it will scream.

These screams will sound different for each of us. Perhaps your body speaks to you through regular headaches or migraines. Maybe back or neck stiffness, digestive issues, skin complaints or unexplained pain is your body's way of getting your attention. Or does your body communicate with you through the physical signs of anxiety or with feeling wakeful in the night?

For over a decade, my body spoke to me in physical pain. Initially, I thought the pain was random, unexplainable, inconvenient and unfair. After years of exploring my pain from both medical and spiritual frameworks, here's what I know to be true. Pain, or other physical sensations, are not random - they are our body's way of communicating with us.

When our body communicates in such strong and extreme ways, it's trying to tell us that we have lost our way. It's urging us to consider the possibility that we have strayed from the path of what really matters; that we have lost connection with our deeper, wiser self.

These physical symptoms are your body's way of letting you know that it's time to come home, to your breath, your heart and your own wisdom and truth.

The problem is, we're not encouraged to listen to our bodies. In fact, quite the opposite. How many of us have been conditioned to ignore our own body's basic cues - hunger, exhaustion, stress or overstimulation? We're taught to push through. We see these bodily cues as inconvenient.

We live in a world that encourages us to operate from the mind. The figure of speech 'a penny for your thoughts' illustrates our habitual desire to get to know what others are thinking above what they are feeling in their bodies or their hearts.

At work, we are asked, 'So what are your thoughts on this project?' In our personal lives, many of us have spent hours trying to think or talk our way out of anxiety, depression, overwhelm or habitual patterns of procrastination, perfectionism, people-pleasing or codependency.

The problem with this mind-centred approach is that humans are 'bottom up' beings. Our body is in the driver's seat, not our mind. Take a moment to consider that 80% of the messages sent through the vagus nerve (our information superhighway) are from the body to the brain whilst only 20% are sent from the brain to the body.

Given that our nervous system's primary function is to keep us safe, when we live from the mind more than the body we are, in essence, ignoring important signals and cues from our body relating to our general wellbeing.

Take a moment now to reflect on the relationship between your mind and your body. Who is in the driver's seat? Who do you listen to and who do you ignore? Does a sense of gratitude, mutual respect and teamwork exist between the two? Or is your body more of a workhorse for your mind, following instruction rather than guiding action?

I know firsthand how challenging it can be to begin to listen to, and trust, your body. When my hands couldn't hold the groceries, when driving the kids to school felt nearly impossible, when exercise left me in pain for days and I felt like there was a sheet of glass separating me from everything and everyone that I loved, it was hard to see my body as anything but an obstruction to my life, a disappointment, something to fix rather than respect.

Perhaps, for you, it's an illness like cancer or an autoimmune disease that's left you feeling let down by your body. Maybe a lifetime of feeling ashamed about how you look has closed you off to the wisdom within?

Or perhaps the pressure to pay the bills has resulted in you living from the mind, pushing on through, sending emails when your neck hurts, sitting for hours at your computer in unhealthy postures, all in the name of productivity, grind and survival.

Given that we are all bottom-up humans, each of us can benefit from learning to listen to our bodies more. Listening to the whispers can be just as illuminating and healing as listening to the screams.

In my mindfulness and meditation community, people with all different issues benefited from opening the lines of communication with their bodies. For example, people who were:

- experiencing migraines, long-COVID, allergies, autoimmune disease, arthritis and high blood pressure.
- suffering from insomnia.
- trying to develop healthy eating and exercise habits.
- injured whilst exercising, playing sport or in car accidents.
- experiencing infertility.
- going through menopause.
- ashamed about how their body looked after operations or treatment.
- aging.

Despite the diversity of experiences, the messages that emerged all contained a similar theme. People were shocked at just how mean, unkind and dismissive they had been towards their bodies over the years. Many people commented on seeing their body as the enemy, a disappointment or a sign of failure. Others reflected on how they had spent a lifetime feeling physically and emotionally cut off from this part of themselves.

Before we learn to connect more deeply with our physical bodies and the wisdom they hold, it's important to note four things.

1. **Don't play the blame game.** This mind-body approach does not imply that if you have an illness or physical ailment that it is your fault! Acknowledging the mind-body connection is not about blaming yourself, it's about connecting to the intelligence of your body and learning to tap into that wisdom to guide your actions moving forward.

2. **Seek support.** Perhaps you have heard the expression 'your issues are stored in your tissues' or 'your body keeps the score'. This relates to implicit memory, the way the body stores past experiences and your responses to these experiences. If you have a history of trauma, please seek the support of a therapist or somatic practitioner as you begin the process of befriending your body, regulating your nervous system, exploring implicit memory and tapping into your body's inherent wisdom.

3. **You've already started.** If opening the lines of communication feels out of your reach, remember you have already been cultivating your capacity to connect with your body throughout this book. All the practices have contained a mind-body element. More specifically, remember in part two we explored how our shadows expressed themselves in our bodies? Also, if you have ever practised mindfulness or meditation, well, chances are, you've already connected to the wisdom held within your body too.

4. **Meditation and medication do mix.** Exploring the mind-body connection doesn't mean you don't need to see a doctor if you have physical symptoms. Opening the lines of communication is a powerful practice in conjunction with medical intervention. It allows for a more holistic approach and can also help you feel more empowered as you navigate the often overwhelming medical system.

So, how do you begin to open the lines of communication?

I started by reflecting upon the qualities of any healthy friendship. Usually these dynamics include mutual respect, asking thoughtful questions, active listening and a genuine desire to help the other person feel seen, heard and appreciated. So, I began, little by little, to create this dynamic with my body.

The following practice is what I used to break the cycle of chronic pain and access the wisdom held within my body.

Try this practice each day for two weeks. You may like to try part one for a few days and then move onto doing part one and two together. After a week, or whenever you are ready, try all three parts together. Remember, friendships based on trust and honesty don't get created overnight, they take time. Be patient as you explore this process.

MINDFUL PRACTICE
BODY WISDOM

Part One:

Begin, as always, in the wholehearted posture. Picture a smile from the expansive sky filtering down into your body and deep into the earth beneath you.

Notice how your miraculous body can both receive and give the essence of a smile. Offer your body a few grateful breaths. Acknowledge all the different ways your body supports you each day.

This body that takes you where you want to go.
These eyes that offer you the gift of flowers in bloom, the changing sky at dusk and dawn, the faces of those you love.
These ears that let you hear laughter, music, rain on the roof and the early morning call of birds.
This mouth that allows you to communicate and to share your perspective, desires and love with family and friends.
These arms and hands that hold, feel and express.
These organs, muscles, tissues, ligaments and bones, all supporting you each and every day.
Every cell that regenerates even whilst you sleep.

Rub your hands together. Notice the friction, the warmth and energy building in the palms of your hands. Place your hands somewhere on your body that feels good for you. Notice the sensation as your hands meet your body.

Repeat a few times: *I am safe in my body. I am safe in my body.*

Notice any experience of relaxation, perhaps your shoulders drop, you sigh or yawn. Trust that in this moment, you are strengthening your relationship with your body.

Part Two:
Repeat a few times: *Body, I appreciate you. I am listening.*
Ask your body: *What message do you have for me? What would you have me know?*
Listen. Notice. Feel. Receive.
Your body may speak to you in words, sensations, emotions, memories or even taste or sound.
Trust any clues that you receive, even if they don't make sense from the position of your mind.
In your own way, thank your body for communicating with you.

Part Three:
Now that you have opened the lines of communication, you may like to deepen the experience by asking your body the following questions:

- How can I better support you?
- What would you like to experience more of?
- What would you like to experience less of?

You may like to write what you discover down and return to it during your day.

Wholehearted confidence includes accessing the wisdom contained in your body and using it to frame your thoughts and actions. When people in my community opened the lines of communication with their bodies, these are some of the messages they received:

- 'The high expectations you place on yourself make your neck sore.'
- 'We are a team. I need you to relax more and worry less.'
- 'It's time to offer my body more kindness.'
- 'Don't push me so hard, it's okay to be gentle with me.'
- 'I am safe to attend to my own needs.'
- 'It's time to view my broken body with love and compassion.'
- 'My body, even though it bears a disease, is not the energy.'
- 'Treat me well and I will do my best for you.'
- 'Start a gratitude practice for your body.'
- 'I'm ready to offer my aging body gratitude and acceptance.'

These messages helped people feel more accepting of how their bodies looked, more grateful for the ways their bodies supported them, and more likely to pause and offer themselves small acts of kindness throughout the day. A glass of water, a quick walk around the block, a stretch of the neck, an early night or a softening of the voice of criticism.

Amazingly, people commented on how, when they began to respect and listen to their bodies more, it felt easier to make healthy choices in relation to food, alcohol, work, technology and social media.

They also shared how this sense of kindness and understanding towards their body filtered out into their relationships, as they noticed themselves feeling more compassionate with friends and family. This is a powerful reminder of how our experience of wholehearted confidence creates positive ripples.

EXPAND

WAKE YOUR HEART GENTLY

I remember when I first 'woke up from the trance of busyness'. I'd been practising mindfulness and meditation consistently for about a year. As I began to break free from the incessant rumination, self-criticism and planning, it felt like life was in high definition. The leaves on the trees seemed brighter, my morning coffee more delicious and my children's laughter especially precious.

There were spontaneous moments of joy that caught me by surprise. Sometimes, a wave of gratitude and wonder would wash over me.

But waking up from the trance also had some unexpected challenges for me. Most notably, as my awareness moved from my head towards my heart, I began to feel things more deeply. Emotions I had buried long ago began to surface at inconvenient times. Seemingly random tears whilst waiting in a supermarket queue – how inopportune! I also noticed myself feeling more compassionate and sensitive to strangers, animals and even trees.

When walking in my neighbourhood, I would see an elderly person with physical limitations and my heart would sink. It was like I was connecting to their vulnerability. Watching short videos on social media about animals would pull my heartstrings in new ways. I read an article about how trees make a noise when they are thirsty, and suddenly my relationship with my indoor plants felt different.

What I hadn't anticipated is that, when you wake up from the trance and commit to living less from your mind and more from your heart, you will *feel* more. More love, joy, gratitude and awe. More compassion, vulnerability, sadness, grief and maybe even anger.

This experience of being surprised by how much I was feeling was not unique to me. I see it play out for people all around the world as they break free from the protective habits of busyness. Only yesterday, I received this message from one of my community members:

'I thought of you this morning as I found myself watching a lizard basking in the sun on a tree trunk. I noticed his little chest expanding and contracting. A tear came to my eye. It was so beautiful watching this little fella's heart beating.'

Whilst beautiful, the sudden opening of our hearts, the ability to see the preciousness of life more clearly, both the joys and the challenges, can for some people feel too much, too soon. So, they return to the safety and predictability of being busy. Their ego reassures them that mindfulness and meditation are best suited to other people, not them. Can you relate?

So, how can we learn to connect more with our hearts, without feeling overwhelmed or tempted to revert to our old, conditioned ways?

As a start, we can remind ourselves that many of the practices in this book have been heart-centred. So, if you have been willing to explore your childhood or your shadows, you have already been connecting with your heart.

If you have experienced gratitude, compassion or forgiveness at any stage throughout the wholehearted confidence journey, you've felt these qualities through the gateway of your heart too. Now let's explore other ways that you can open your heart gently.

EXPAND

VISUALISATION PRACTICE
PULLING WEEDS &
PLANTING SEEDS

If your heart has been quiet and small, living beneath the protective layers of self-criticism, judgement towards others or just a generalised feeling of detachment or separation, soften the layers slowly. You can do this by giving your heart one thing to focus on each day, so it feels safe.

Try the following practice for seven days as you begin to awaken your heart to its full potential.

Begin as always in the wholehearted posture. Now for one minute, imagine that as you breathe in, you are filling your heart with fresh oxygen. Trust that as you focus your attention in your heart space, you are gently waking your heart. You might notice your shoulders relax, your breath slow or a feeling of ease or warmth.

Imagine that, with each breath, you are softening the protective layers around your heart caused by busyness, regrets and disappointment from your past and the fears for your future.

Imagine that, within your heart, there is a garden. Notice the trees, shrubs and flowers. Notice also the weeds. These weeds represent harsh judgement, self-criticism, blame, control, rumination, regret, disappointment and so on - all the qualities that keep your heart small.

Pick one weed (for example, 'blame') and imagine pulling it from the garden of your heart. Make a commitment to pulling this weed each time you notice it today.

Now, move your awareness to the rich soil in your garden, filled with nutrients, minerals, bugs and earthworms. Notice that within this soil there are many different seeds. You can see seeds of compassion, forgiveness, gratitude, respect, acceptance, dignity, trust, hope, vitality, purpose and so on.

Pick one seed, and in your mind's eye, imagine giving it everything it needs to germinate - water, the right temperature and sunlight. Notice it breaking through the soil. Make a commitment to growing this seed as you move through your day.

Turn this practice into an intention. For example: *Today I pull the weeds of blame and plant the seeds of trust.*

Repeat this intention a few times silently in your mind. You may also like to write it in your journal or on a Post-it Note on your computer so you can refer back to it throughout your day.

Well done. You have just allowed your heart to show you what it would like to move away from and towards today. Keep this heart wisdom alive today and use it to shape your thoughts and guide your actions.

MOVING FROM YOUR HEAD TO YOUR HEART

When we operate primarily from our mind, we often get caught in conditioned egoic responses. Judgement. Blame. Criticism. Regret. Rumination. We get frustrated when people change plans because that's what we always do. We worry about work because it feels normal to do so. We criticise our efforts or actions out of habit.

When we learn to tap into the intelligence of our hearts, we can make decisions that are less habitual, fresher, more creative and loving. When plans change, we are more able to go with the flow. When worry surfaces, we can offer ourselves compassion and perspective. When our inner voice becomes critical, we can respond with friendliness and warmth.

Science is only just beginning to confirm what spiritual traditions have been teaching for thousands of years - that the heart contains an intelligence that influences the mind, personality, our capacity to connect with non-local information and to make wise and skilful decisions.

The founders of the HeartMath Institute, Doc Childre and Howard Martin, collated over thirty years of research in their book, *The HeartMath Solution*. Their goal is to bridge the gap between spirituality and science and to make living from the heart more accessible and common.

Here are five facts they share as a way of inviting people to expand their understanding and appreciation of the heart:

1. The heart contains its own independent nervous system, comprising more than 40,000 neurons.

2. The heart is the body's master oscillator. The rhythm of the heart pulls all the body's systems into a state of entrainment or synchronisation.

3. The heart produces the largest rhythmic electromagnetic field of any of the body's organs. Its electrical field is about sixty times greater in amplitude than the electrical activity generated by the brain.

4. You can use your heart to regulate your nervous system. By intentionally cultivating feelings of love, appreciation and compassion you can down-regulate the sympathetic nervous system (fight or flight) and increase the activity of the parasympathetic nervous system (rest and digest).

5. Through your heart, you can learn to connect with information that lives beyond the memories and knowledge held in your mind. You can also access information beyond what you can see, feel and experience in your immediate environment.

After reading these facts, do you feel more inspired to take the time each day to move from your head to your heart? If so, you can begin with one of my favourite practices – the heartful pause.

MINDFUL PRACTICE
THE HEARTFUL PAUSE

You can pause at any time during your day and try this practice. Begin by taking a few deep and intentional breaths. Imagine that with each breath, you are waking your heart. Now ask yourself: *Am I operating from my head or my heart right now?*

The answer may come to you in the form of a word, a physical sensation, a memory or just a knowing. (If nothing comes up, assume that you are operating from your mind and continue with the steps outlined below.)

If you received a sign that you are already operating from your heart, offer yourself a smile and spend a few minutes lingering in this moment. Feel any warmth within your chest, relaxation within your body or calm within your mind. Trust that as you linger here, you are creating a positive feedback loop where your heart feels appreciated. This will strengthen your ability to access states like love, compassion, forgiveness, peace and perspective as you move through your day.

If you realised that you are operating from the mind, gently place your hand on your heart. As you breathe, feel your hand rise and fall on your chest. Notice any relaxation spread across your body as you do this.

Repeat a few times silently: *I connect to the wisdom contained in my heart. I allow my heart to guide my actions.* Take a few more deep breaths.

Now enquire: *What would acting from my heart look like in this moment?*

Trust whatever wisdom, advice or suggestion comes forward. Take heartfelt action.

CONFIDENCE IN ACTION –
THE HEART'S INNER LANDSCAPE

Rita is in her seventies. She lives in Puerto Rico. She has survived cancer, and more recently, Hurricane Fiona that swept across her island. Her life has certainly had its challenges. Through these, Rita has stayed open and loving, to herself, her family and her home.

Rita was very committed to the wholehearted confidence experience. She moved beyond the language barriers and also found a way to email her responses even when there was no power or electricity. She communicated with me and listened to all the meditations even when feeling unwell with her cancer medication.

During the wholehearted confidence experience, Rita created a powerful image of her heart. She shared, 'I imagine that within my heart there is a forest with huge, thousand-year-old trees. There are mountains and lots of vegetation and many gardens. Within my heart there are also lakes, waterfalls and deep caves. Many animals inhabit the forest within my heart. From the top of the mountains, I can see the sea.'

Rita learnt to connect with her heart during challenging times. When she found herself awake at night, or sitting in the doctor's waiting room, she closed her eyes and imagined the world inside her heart.

In her mind's eye, she would explore the forest and its old trees with a sense of calm. Within the landscape of her heart Rita learnt to connect with her inner strength and sense of eternal peace. She carried this with her, allowing it to relax her in the challenging moments and enliven her during the happy times.

EXPAND

Has Rita's story encouraged you to create a sanctuary within your heart – a place you can go to feel calm and peaceful?

ALLOW YOUR EMOTIONS

Whilst the idea of feeling your feelings may appear obvious, many of us avoid, ignore or squash down our emotions. Or we get in the habit of talking about our feelings, analysing and intellectualising them rather than experiencing them in our bodies and hearts.

These habits of resistance often stem from our childhood. Perhaps, when you were growing up there were emotions that were acceptable, like joy and happiness, and others that you weren't allowed to express, like anger or jealousy.

Maybe, as an adult, you experience a more constant, low-level emotional experience that impacts how you see the world, like vigilance or anticipation. Perhaps, deep within your heart, under layers of protection, there is grief or sadness desperately wanting to be expressed.

There are many different theories about emotions, how many we have, whether they are basic or complex, universal or context based, and their effects on our psychology, physiology, our outlook and our actions. Whilst there isn't scope in this book to explore these different theories in detail, it's worth noting four contentions offered by different experts (Jill Bolte-Taylor, John Bradshaw, Robert Plutchik and Eckhart Tolle, respectively).

EXPAND

1. The physiological lifespan of an emotion in the body and brain is ninety seconds. This means that the pure expression of an emotion will come and go quite quickly. It's the resistance and the stories we attach to the emotion that stay around for longer.

2. Emotions are energy in motion and if they are not expressed, the energy is repressed.

3. If emotions are left unchecked, they can intensify. For example, annoyance can transform into anger and then into rage.

4. If you are cut off from your emotions, you will eventually experience them on a purely physical level, as a physical problem or symptom.

Obviously, this doesn't mean that, if you are experiencing an emotion like grief, the experience will only last ninety seconds. It will continue to cycle through your body as many times as it needs to.

Trust that each time you attend to the somatic experience of grief (or any other emotion), you are sending a powerful message to your body and heart that you are listening, respecting and honouring them.

Cultivating your capacity to attend to what is here in the moment, to not push anything away, will help you to feel more resilient, empowered and confident. If you would like further support in exploring your emotions, please contact a trained professional.

With these ideas in mind, you can begin to attend to your emotions by exploring this five-step process.

1. **Become familiar with the wide range of human emotions.** For example, joy, love, happiness, acceptance, surprise, awe, appreciation, vigilance, anticipation, sadness, fear, grief, shame, guilt, loathing, disgust, anger and rage. Remind yourself that every emotion serves a purpose and that there are no good or bad emotions. Set yourself the intention to notice your emotions as you move through your day in a way that feels safe for you and others.

2. **Let go of your stories.** When you notice an emotion arise, take a deep breath, unhook from any stories and move your awareness into your body. Allow the emotion to express itself in your body without the usual accompanying narratives.

3. **Become the witness to sensation.** Remind yourself that emotions move through the body in ninety seconds. Breathe. Notice physical sensations.

4. **Trust.** Repeat silently in your mind: *Emotions come and go like clouds in the sky. I am safe to feel my emotions.*

5. **Find a feeling of safety.** Scan your body for any places that feel relaxed or at ease. Rest your attention here for a few breaths as a way to recalibrate. Or you can settle into the wholehearted posture if you prefer.

When people within my community committed to waking their hearts gently, taking heartfelt pauses during their days and allowing their emotions, they got in touch with a deeper wisdom within. Here are some of the ways it felt and what they discovered:

How it felt:

- 'It was so reassuring to know that I can connect with this peaceful place within me whenever I need to.'
- 'A wave of relief washed over me.'
- 'It was a deeply emotional experience. I cried tears of acknowledgement for just how hard the last few years have been.'
- 'It's so empowering to know that I am brave enough to sit with emotions I have avoided for years'.
- 'Like meeting an old friend, it felt so comfortable.'

What they discovered:

- 'My heart can cut through the haze of my mind and reveal to me what really matters.'
- 'Through the heart, I can accept all aspects of me, including the parts I have long felt ashamed of.'
- 'My heart always whispers something loving, exactly what I need in the moment.'
- 'When I make decisions from my heart, I feel more calm, grounded and confident.'
- 'My heart often encourages me to rest.'
- 'Through the pathway of the heart, regrets and past mistakes feel smaller.'
- It's time to end an unhealthy friendship.'
- 'It's okay to accept my life stage.'
- 'Boundaries are healthy for everyone.'
- 'Stay in the present moment, and all will be well.'

Remember, your heart is available as a source of wisdom and intelligence anytime you need it. You can call upon it to relax you in stressful situations, soothe you when you are feeling self-critical, or guide you to make wise and skilful decisions.

NATURE SPEAKS. ARE YOU LISTENING?

We take a weekend walk in nature and pause to enjoy an elevated view. Looking down, we observe the treetops gently swaying in the wind. We can hear the sound of water moving across smooth river rocks in a stream nearby. In this moment, we are open and receptive to the natural ebb and flow of life.

From this vantage point, it feels easy to let go of our little worries, the narratives we hold about who is right and who is wrong, and our expectations about how our lives are supposed to look and feel.

We tilt our heads towards the night sky and suddenly that new stain on the carpet, those shoes we've been desiring, the kilos we want to lose, fade into insignificance. We feel the warm sun land on our backs, or the cool breeze meet our skin, and for a moment, time stops. There is no need to strive, push or grind. In this moment we *have* enough. We *are* enough.

Nature cracks us open in both subtle and surprising ways. As Rob (from part two of this book) reflected:

> *'Whether it's noticing the expansive beauty of a sunset or unique cloud formations, to seeing a caterpillar inch along in its magical heaving pattern of movement, the natural world keeps me grounded and humble.*

EXPAND

I often find myself amazed. Sometimes this sense of amazement feels like the surprise and awe of a child, other times it comes from a place of deep appreciation, gratitude and reverence I have nurtured as a grown man.'

Science supports what we know deep within our being – nature offers us the gifts of humility, perspective, peace, connection, awe and wonder, balance and hope. Just like an old friend who knows us intimately, nature always finds a way to give us just what we need and desire, even without us asking.

Wholehearted confidence invites us to take our relationship with nature to a deeper level. We do this not by travelling to far-off destinations or embarking on epic off-the-grid adventures, but rather, by opening the lines of communication with the natural world (just as we have done with our bodies and our hearts).

So how do you begin? It's really quite simple. Go outside once a day and intentionally cultivate a mindful moment. Engage your senses. What colours, textures or natural features do you observe?

Can you hear birds, the wind rustling through the trees, a dog barking in the distance or crunchy autumn leaves beneath your feet?

Allow your fingertips to move across the textured bark on a tree or the soft petals of a flower. Take a few deep breaths. Linger with gentle curiosity. Notice the sense of aliveness all around you.

Take another few breaths into your heart. Ask: *Nature, what message do you have for me? What wisdom can you share?*

And just as you did with your body and your heart, listen, open and receive. Trust that nature may speak to you with words or a feeling. It might offer you wisdom through a falling leaf, a flock of birds moving across the sky or a snail leaving its silver wake across the pavement.

Within my international community, many people commented on how different it felt to see nature as a source of wisdom rather than just something to enjoy. They also reflected upon how knowing that there was a powerful source of intelligence out there that they could access anytime increased their experience of wholehearted confidence.

My community began to open the lines of communication by connecting with the season they were in and opening to any wisdom it held. Just like the body and the heart, nature had a lot to say! Here is what she communicated to different members of my research group:

SUMMER

- It's time to start that creative project.
- Host a dinner party.
- Care less about what others think of you.
- Move your body every day.
- Drink more water.
- Celebrate how far you have come.
- It's okay to be happy.
- Make more of an effort to see the sunset.
- Eat dinner outside.
- Take your shoes off and feel the grass beneath your feet.
- Laugh more, don't take yourself so seriously.

AUTUMN

- Let go of the mistakes from your past.
- Offer yourself compassion.
- Create healthy boundaries.
- Practise saying no.
- Let go of that toxic relationship.
- Trust your ability to make decisions.
- Go at a slower pace.

WINTER

- It's okay to rest.
- Return to your meditation practice.
- Start making more soups.
- This too shall pass.
- Everything changes.
- You are safe.
- Go to bed early.
- Journal.
- Make time for your old friends.

SPRING

- Move your body a little each day.
- Cultivate hope.
- Practise gratitude.
- Be patient.
- Plan a mini break.
- Listen to live music.
- Communicate more from the heart.
- Spend more time in nature.
- Trust the cycles of life.

MOVE YOUR BODY EVERY DAY

BRATE HOW FAR YOU HAVE COME

IT'S OKAY TO BE HAPPY

E LESS ABOUT WHAT OTHERS THINK OF YOU

CONFIDENCE IN ACTION -
THE SEASON OF LETTING GO

You might remember Ava, the woman who in part three experienced a powerful moment of appreciation with a teacher she supports in Indonesia. This sense of appreciation continued as Ava connected deeply with the season of autumn in Japan.

Ava imagined herself as a strong and wise tree. With every falling leaf, she was able to connect with past hurts she was now ready to let go. As her past fell gently to the earth below, she felt the relief of letting go. She then pictured these aspects of her life nourishing the soil as they decomposed.

'In this way everything has a purpose, nothing is wasted. My challenges, like the decomposing leaves, nourish my future self,' she explained.

Ava continued to reflect, 'This theme of letting go of hurts has been strong over the last two weeks. A lot of old memories that became grudges and resentments have resurfaced. Each time one came up I thought of it as a falling leaf and let the pain associated with it go, but I kept the memory and the lesson it carried to become part of my story.

'To keep the wisdom and ditch the pain. I realised I've experienced a lot in my life and instead of feeling hard done by, I began to feel grateful for having so many rich opportunities to understand what it means to be human. Feeling compassion for people I deeply resented for years is so liberating.'

How do you feel about the possibility of allowing the wisdom from your past hurts to feed and nurture you? Is there one small aspect of your past that you can 'keep the wisdom but ditch the pain' like Ava did?

CELEBRATING OUR SEASONS

Nature's seasons remind us of our own seasons. As humans, there will be times when our energy is high and we feel naturally creative, in flow and social. There will also be times when our energy is low and our body asks us to rest. There will be moments when we feel stuck and heavy, and moments of great transition and growth.

Whilst nature moves through her seasons with ease and grace, many of us resist our cycles, and as a consequence, we suffer. As we walk the wholehearted confidence path, we allow nature to teach us to rise and fall with the natural ebb and flow of life.

Some of the cycles you may move through include:

- Letting go.
- Surrendering.
- Resting.
- Hibernating.
- Forgiving.
- Healing.
- Planning.
- Hustling.
- Celebrating.
- Socialising.
- Creating.
- Expanding.
- Maintaining.

HONOURING YOUR CYCLES

What I've learnt from working with people all around the world is that most of us feel comfortable with certain cycles and uncomfortable with others. We find pleasure in some and pain in others. Over time, it's this getting pulled into and away from, that causes suffering, not the cycles themselves.

Take a moment to read over the previous list and just notice how you feel about these different cycles. Are there some that you really enjoy or feel naturally comfortable in? Are there some that are your default way of moving through the world? Are there others that you don't value, resist or even fear?

Within my community, I've noticed two cycles that people habitually resist or sabotage, and as a consequence, their inner confidence suffers. These are rest and creativity. Let's explore them together now.

WELCOMING REST

In our culture of productivity, grind and hustle, many of us see rest as a waste of time, boring or a sign of weakness or laziness.

There have been two times in my life that I have been 100% committed to resisting rest (and in case you were wondering, this strategy didn't work well for me!).

The first was when I was in the throes of my chronic pain condition, and the second was during my COVID-19 recovery. In both instances, my body sent a clear message to me that every afternoon I needed to have a nap. My ego didn't like this at all. It said things to me like, *You are in the prime of your life, you've got interesting work to do, ideas to be shared, now is not the time for a nap.*

Sometimes, my ego got creative and spoke to me through a persistent cloud of anxiety it had generated. A heaviness across my chest, a tightness within my gut, a nondescript feeling of impending doom. I certainly didn't feel like taking a nap in that state! Underneath the anxiety was a deep belief that, if I rested, I wouldn't be able to do all the things I needed to do to be a good mother and meditation teacher.

Can you relate to this story? Has there been a time in your life, perhaps due to illness, injury or just a life stage when your body has told you it needed rest, and you have resisted? How did the resistance express itself for you?

The truth is, when we ignore our body's calls for rest, we suffer. We become more tired, anxious, depleted or overwhelmed. In some cases, we get very sick.

As Eckhart Tolle explains in *The Power of Now:*

> 'Many illnesses are created through fighting against the cycles of low energy, which are vital for regeneration. The compulsion to do, and the tendency to derive our sense of self-worth and identity from external factors such as achievement make us resist the low cycles rather than surrender into them. In these circumstances, the intelligence of our body may take over as a self-protective measure and create an illness in order to force us to stop so that the necessary regeneration takes place.'

We are once more reminded that, if we don't listen to the whispers, our body will scream.

Before moving on, take a moment to consider how you could begin to honour your body's need for rest as part of the wholehearted confidence journey.

Could you commit to going to bed a little earlier? Could you resist the urge to pack your weekends full and instead leave an afternoon free? Perhaps, before you grab that afternoon coffee, you could have a mindful moment, breathing deeply, engaging your senses and relaxing your body?

BEING CREATIVE

As humans, we are all inherently creative. This doesn't mean that you need to be able to draw or paint. Creativity, when understood from a more spiritual perspective, is less about producing art and more about cultivating your capacity to live in flow and to receive the sense of aliveness held in the present moment.

Perhaps, for you, creativity comes in the form of cooking, gardening, dancing or telling stories. Maybe, you express your creativity through problem-solving or finding ways to make your routine more fun and interesting. Walking a different way to the train station, breaking an unhealthy dynamic with your children, learning to respond to your ego in different ways – these can all be expressions of creativity.

Many people in my community have a deep desire to express themselves more fully. They are keen to learn a language, try a pottery class or write a book. They want to say 'yes' to the inner rumblings, to a life that feels less productive and more expressive, free flowing, purposeful and inspired.

For so many of these people, the cycle of creativity gets dampened by the ego. It whispers things like 'you are too old to try something new' or 'you aren't the creative one in your family' or 'people will judge you'.

I've seen on many occasions what transpires when people get hooked into the story of their ego. The creative energy gets suppressed and they suffer. For some, it feels like flatness or stuckness. For others, it expresses itself as a sinking feeling, a deep knowing that they aren't making the most of their lives or living their full potential.

Take a moment to think back to the last time you wanted to try something new and your ego got in the way, convincing you it wasn't a good idea. How did you feel when you dampened your natural creative flow? Heavy. Stuck. Flat. Disappointed. Self-critical. Small. Resentful. How could you better support yourself next time you receive creative inspiration?

Our internal cycles will come and go just like the seasons in nature. Just as you probably have a favourite season, there are no doubt cycles that you enjoy more than others too. The question is, can you embrace them all, without getting pulled in by comfort or pleasure, or turned off by discomfort or pain?

INTUITION FOR YOU, ME & EVERYBODY

It's easy to assume that only certain people are intuitive, or that it's a practice best suited to spiritual people, tarot readers, energy healers, meditation teachers and so on.

In truth, we all have the capacity to connect with our intuition. In my community I've witnessed teachers, artists, doctors, IT consultants, students, managers, pilots, photographers, nurses and physiotherapists all harness this ability and use it to live a life with greater meaning, purpose and intention.

Whilst there are many different ways of understanding intuition, a simple definition I find most helpful is: *the ability to access information beyond what is held in the mind or can be accessed in the immediate environment.*

Perhaps, as a parent, you can remember a time when you knew that a friendship or romantic relationship your child was in wasn't going to end well, and then sure enough, there was a breakup, hurt and disappointment.

Maybe, sometimes you just have a feeling that you need to attend an event, sign up for a course or contact a friend, and when you do, more information surfaces and you know it was the right decision. Or do you use your sense of knowing at work to direct projects, engage teams or communicate?

Whilst the word intuition hasn't been used once in this book (this was intentional!), I hope you are coming to understand that, as you open the lines of communication with your younger self, your shadows, body, heart, cycles and mother nature, you are harnessing your intuition.

Many times throughout this book you've been asked to connect with intelligence that lives beyond your rational mind, your memory or the information you can access in your environment.

When it comes to wholehearted confidence, however, what is more important than accessing your intuition is cultivating your capacity to trust it and act from this wisdom.

I remember a delightful student who was earnest and committed. She shared with me how, every time she tried to access her intuition, nothing happened. I asked her to elaborate. She explained how, when she asked nature for a sign, all she saw was a rainbow.

I smiled and asked, 'Do you think that beautiful display of colour and light in the sky may have been a clue for you?' To which she replied, 'Oh, I thought it needed to be something more obvious than a rainbow.' Aren't us humans funny sometimes?

Harnessing your intuition is about noticing the big, small and sometimes subtle signs that life offers you. The sudden desire to call an old friend. A bird that comes to visit each morning. A flutter in your heart. A song. A memory.

It's about trusting in what you notice and opening to the deeper meaning. And finally, it includes daring to use these signs, feelings or wisdom to guide your actions. For example, calling that friend, listening to the words of the song and relating them to your own life, getting curious about why that memory is resurfacing. Is it asking you to forgive, move on or notice a reoccurring pattern in your life?

As we come to the end of our discussion about opening the lines of communication between our bodies, hearts, natural world, cycles and seasons, I hope you are starting to believe - to *know* - that there is a wealth of information, guidance, love, peace and perspective available within and around you.

Calling upon this vast pool of intelligence will help you feel more comfortable in your own skin, grounded within your heart and at home in the world.

IMPERMANENCE - THE HEART OF REALITY

By now, you will be getting a sense that every aspect of life is impermanent. Our emotions, inner narratives and relationships. The life cycle of a star, tree, animal, disease, political system or nation. They are all in a constant state of transformation.

Take a moment to consider how this makes you feel. Anxious, heavy, relieved, hopeful? Something else?

When people first come to meditation or the practice of looking inwards, they often feel resistant to the idea that life is always changing. They cling onto the way things used to be or to their ideas about what the future should look and feel like. Over time, however, people soften and see the beauty contained in the reality of change and transformation.

Impermanence as a Buddhist teaching invites us to let go of our habitual desire to control life, and instead, to soften into the truth that the changing nature of life can be beautiful, and that we can feel safe within it.

As Thich Nhat Hanh explains in *The Art of Living:*

> *'Contemplating impermanence helps us to touch freedom and happiness in the present moment. It helps us see reality as it is, so we can embrace change, face our fears and cherish what we have. When we can see the impermanent nature of a flower, the person we love, our own body, our pain and sorrow, we can make a breakthrough into the heart of reality.'*

Next time you get caught inside your mind, wanting to cling onto the way things are, take a deep breath into your heart and remind yourself gently that impermanence is what makes life possible. Without it, the sun would not rise and offer us the gift of light and life. Our garden would not flower in spring. Our children would not grow into adults. Our creative endeavours would never come to life. We ourselves would not learn, grow or heal.

Spiritual teachers such as Tara Brach and Jack Kornfield often refer to mindfulness as being like a bird that needs two wings to fly. These wings are wisdom and compassion. I like to use this bird metaphor to explore the power of embracing impermanence too. We can imagine that one wing represents how impermanence can help us be with our challenges in more open and loving ways. The other wing can relate to cherishing all we have and allowing impermanence to help us to act in more courageous, intentional and wholehearted ways. Let's explore these two wings of impermanence together now.

VISUALISATION PRACTICE ON THE WINGS OF A BIRD

Take a few breaths in the wholehearted posture. Imagine that you are sitting somewhere at first light. The sun is peeking just over the horizon line. Hues of dusty pink transform into burnt orange. Streaks of lilac meet splashes of lemon.

You notice a bird flying across the morning sky. It knows exactly when to exert effort and when to glide. It's such a beautiful example of taking the path of least resistance, of working with your natural environment and going with the flow.

You wonder what your life would look and feel like if you embodied these qualities more often - if you could resist and control less, and trust more.

The bird comes closer, and in a moment that fills you with delight and surprise, it lands next to you.

You look at this bird with the eyes of a child, filled with wonder and intrigue. You notice the small details on its feathers, its perfect eyes, even its feet seem beautiful.

Somehow you know that this bird is here to help you trust the natural ebb and flow of life, to feel comfortable amidst the constant change.

You remember the two wings of impermanence and ask this bird these questions:

1. How can I allow impermanence to help me through hard times?
2. How can impermanence help me feel more wholeheartedly confident?

You listen. Receive. Trust.

WHeN I
reMeMBeR
the
imPermanENt
nAtuRe of
liFe,
mY tRouBles
feeL sMaller

I can care for you,
but I cannot take away
your suffering

I can teach you,
but I cannot control
your actions

HOW TO CARE WHOLEHEARTEDLY

If you are still here, reading this book about wholehearted confidence, chances are you have a natural capacity for compassion and a genuine care for others. Maybe, within your family or friendship group, you are known as the kind one or the person always willing to lend a hand. Perhaps, you care deeply about the injustices in the world or the state of your local community.

It's also likely that sometimes, this care for others, or for humanity, can leave you feeling shaken or wobbly, like a tree without roots being blown about by the wind and the rain.

Perhaps, when your child is going through a rough patch, you feel it deeply. You lie in bed at night worrying, problem-solving or ruminating, whilst your partner is sound asleep beside you. Maybe seeing your parents face health challenges as they age affects you more than it does your siblings. Or has witnessing a friend go through cancer left its mark?

So, how can you care, but not feel so thrown about by your concern? How can you learn to calibrate your actions and feelings?

By learning to balance your natural sense of compassion with equanimity, you will feel more grounded and balanced whilst supporting those you care about. In Buddhist traditions, compassion and equanimity are two of the Four Virtues of the Heart. Let's explore them together now.

EXPAND

COMPASSION, UNCALIBRATED

Compassion is the inner quality that allows us to be with the suffering of others and to act from the desire to reduce this suffering. If we don't learn to calibrate our compassion, we can feel overwhelmed by the plight of others, deeply emotional or exhausted. Perhaps you can think back to a time when your compassion felt uncalibrated, a period when you were really pulled in by someone else's life?

Sharon Salzberg describes equanimity as 'a spacious stillness that can accept things as they are'. This value of the heart can help to calibrate our compassion, by acting like a buffer, allowing us to open to all aspects of life, without feeling so thrown about.

We can be with the suffering, both our own and of others, with courage and openness, but without getting so pulled in. We can care but not get overwhelmed because of that care. And when we can move through the world in this way, we feel wholeheartedly confident.

Is there someone in your life right now who you would like to feel more equanimity towards?

Within my meditation and mindfulness community, people have explored balancing compassion and equanimity in relation to:

- Caring for aging parents.
- Supporting children who are being bullied at school.
- Nursing sick partners.
- Supporting adult children who are facing challenges like drug addiction, alcoholism, financial stress and divorce.

- Raising kids with neurodiversity.
- Taking a step back at work.
- Supporting friends with cancer.
- Supporting siblings going through divorce or financial hardship.

As with many of the practices in this book, learning to practise equanimity sounds good on paper, but in reality, when we attempt to calibrate our care, we will meet with all sorts of resistance.

Our egos will chime in, saying things like, *You're their mother, it's your job to do everything you can to help.* Our shadows will appear, revealing childhood conditioning that whispers, *You must attend to the needs of your parents above your own.* Or the high expectations you place on yourself may creep in, as you attempt to be perfect in your role as carer or support person to a friend in need.

The good news is that you already have lots of experience being with your resistance. You know how to befriend it, how to notice its expression in your body and the thoughts it generates. You also know when to offer it your warm-hearted curiosity and when to stand firm and say *not now*.

IS BUSYNESS YOUR SECURITY BLANKET?

If we desire to feel less pulled into the tide of other people's lives, we also need to become aware of the protective quality that 'getting busy helping' contains. When our attention is consumed by baking lasagna for our friend who is unwell, or by calling yet another allied health professional for our aging parents, we are, to some degree, protecting ourselves from the deeper feelings of grief and sadness.

When we get consumed by offering suggestions to our adult children about books they can read or courses they can take to help them navigate their challenges, we are protecting ourselves from the undercurrent of helplessness we feel.

When we soften our habits of busyness, we are forced to feel what lies beneath. We are also invited to acknowledge the deeper truth, that despite our best intentions, we cannot make things better for those we love. We cannot take away their pain or carry their burdens for them. It is their life to walk, not ours.

Whilst difficult, when we acknowledge these truths, we simultaneously open to the possibility of witnessing the strength and resilience of those we care about. When we let go, we create space for others to find their own solutions. Through our surrender, we get to witness those we love and care about find meaning in their own challenges. Over time, we may even be able to see our equanimity as a gift to those we love.

The path towards greater equanimity may feel messy, and at times, painful. It's okay to take it slow. You may also like to begin by exploring the practice with someone who you feel neutral towards or fond of, rather than someone who you love deeply.

MINDFUL PRACTICE
SPACIOUS CARE

Begin with the wholehearted posture. Take a few deep breaths with your shoulders back and your heart open.

Think about someone in your life who you would like to feel a greater experience of equanimity towards. Perhaps this person is your child, parent, sibling or friend. You can also choose someone neutral if that feels more comfortable. Trust yourself here.

Picture this person in your mind's eye. Notice the clothes they like to wear, their posture, what they enjoy doing. Take some time to think about the challenges they are facing or the circumstances of their life right now.

As you do this, acknowledge the ways you get pulled in by these challenges. Do you get busy trying to help? Do you offer solutions? Do you feel anxious, distracted or overwhelmed? Do you feel this uncalibrated care as a heaviness in your heart?

Focus on your exhale. With each exhale, notice a softening in your body. As you breathe out, imagine letting go of these feelings of being pulled in.

Notice any resistance that may come up. Continue to focus on your outbreath and this feeling of letting go. Feel your feet steady on the ground.

Offer this person the phrases below. Repeat them silently in your mind (you may like to place your hand on your heart as you do).

> *I care about you and your challenges, but I cannot make your troubles go away.*
>
> *I can care for you, but I cannot take away your suffering.*
>
> *I can teach you, but I cannot control your actions.*
>
> *See my equanimity as a gift, an opportunity for you to find your own solutions and resilience.*
>
> *I offer my love, and I trust that you will find meaning in your challenges.*

If there is one phrase that resonates with you, repeat it a few more times. Notice emotions come and go. Notice resistance. Let it all ebb and flow.

Well done. You can use this practice anytime you notice yourself feeling pulled in or ungrounded by your desire to help or your care for others. Remember, balancing compassion and equanimity isn't about becoming cold and unfeeling, it's about calibrating our responses so that we may feel strong and spacious amidst our care.

CONFIDENCE IN ACTION - LETTERS TO MY CHILDREN

Louise has four adult sons. She has always been a devoted mother. When the boys were young, she was hands-on, driving them to endless sporting events, cooking their favourite meals and generally trying her best to offer them a great start in life.

Now, as adults, Louise's four boys are making big decisions about their careers, partners and life direction without her. Intellectually, Louise knows that this separation is normal, natural and healthy, but in her heart, there exists a sadness and some resistance.

Louise began practising mindfulness later in life to help her feel more present to her emotions, accepting of her life stage and compassionate towards her younger self.

During the wholehearted confidence experience, Louise noticed how, at times, she felt the urge to influence the direction of her children's lives. Like so many mothers, sometimes she got caught in the belief that she knew what was best for her sons more than they did. At the same time, she was aware that her role was now one of support and witnessing rather than directing.

As a way of exploring these natural but contradictory feelings, Louise wrote each of her sons a letter. In these letters, she shared all the ways she was proud of her boys. She explained to each of her sons that she trusted them to make their own decisions as adults. Louise described this process as 'setting her boys free'.

Louise has no intention of sending these letters to her sons. The process was for her. It was an opportunity for Louise to rest in the spacious awareness of equanimity, where we can care, but not feel pulled in by the care. Louise feels pleased to have these letters to refer back to when she notices herself feeling pulled in from time to time, as most mothers do!

I'm curious, if you wrote a letter etched with the energy of letting go and equanimity, who would you address it to?

EXPAND

ACCEPTING LIFE AS IT IS

We all know the story of our challenges so intimately. We can recall the details perfectly. The moments when we were let down by those we love. Our own regrettable actions. The injustice of it all. The remorse, regret and resistance etched into every cell in our bodies.

What if we could invite equanimity to hold us in these moments, to soften our critical mind and our heavy hearts? What if we could allow this sense of spacious stillness to cradle the regrets from our past, the fears for our future and the challenges of today, so that we could feel more grounded and at ease?

We can all use the practice of equanimity to help us in different aspects of our lives. In my community, people explored equanimity to:

- Feel less judgemental about the way they've been treated in the past.
- Feel more empowered and less like a victim.
- Forgive themselves for being an absent parent to their young children.
- Create space between themselves and their fears for their children's future.
- Take their marriage breakup less personally.
- Forgive friends who let them down.

I wonder what aspects of your life you could hold in a more spacious awareness? Let's find out together.

It feels good to place the circumstances of my life in the vast ocean of awareness

VISUALISATION PRACTICE
THE OCEAN OF
AWARENESS

Take three breaths in the wholehearted posture. Imagine that you are sitting on a beach on a perfect day. The sun's rays feel just right. A gentle breeze meets your skin. You feel relaxed and at ease.

Sitting here on the water's edge you reflect upon a story, event or circumstance that you hold tight about your life. Maybe, it's a narrative about your past, a time you were let down, experienced pain or acted in regrettable ways. Perhaps, the story relates to a current-day issue or a concern for your future.

Picture yourself holding a little bucket filled with water - the type that children use to make sandcastles on the beach. Using your imagination, place this story, event or circumstance in the bucket.

Notice how the water level rises with its weight. Notice also how this story feels constrained and stuck in this small container. It has little room to move, transform or dissipate.

Now look out to the ocean. Scan your eyes across the horizon line. Take a few deep breaths as you really acknowledge how vast and deep the water is. Always moving and changing. Imagine for a moment how different this narrative of yours would feel if it had the space to move freely within this large body of water.

Picture yourself walking over to the water's edge. You can feel the cool water touch your feet. In your own way, place this story, event or circumstance in the ocean. Watch it drift out, past the wave break, into the depths of the ocean. Take delight in seeing this story bobbing about, moving with the tide. Notice how free it looks. It has room to move, change shape and transform.

Become aware of how good it feels to place the circumstances of your life in the vast ocean of awareness. Do your challenges feel smaller? Do you feel less pulled in or reactive?

Sit a moment longer, feeling grateful for your ability to cultivate equanimity, to feel less burdened and more free.

REFRAMING OUR PAIN

Now that we have practised placing certain events or circumstances in the vast sea of awareness (as a way of feeling more open and less pulled in), we are ready to explore our pain (emotional, physical, mental, spiritual, financial) with this same sense of spaciousness.

Before we do, a word or two about 'spiritual bypassing'. The term was first coined in the 1980s by transpersonal psychotherapist John Welwood in *Towards a Psychology of Awakening*. It relates to our tendency to use spiritual ideas and practices to avoid facing our emotions and psychological wounds.

In relation to responding to pain or challenges, spiritual bypassing may present as looking for the silver linings before you have sat with the emotional aspect of your pain. It may include seeing your pain as a learning opportunity first and foremost and disregarding the psychological scars or impact.

Often phrases like 'everything happens for a reason', 'it was a blessing in disguise' or 'trust in the universe' contain the energy of spiritual bypassing.

So, with this awareness, it's worth noting that the practice I shall discuss here isn't the first approach you would take when a challenge comes your way. It is a tool you may like to explore only once you have honoured your emotional landscape, and if needed, accessed the support of a trained professional.

EXPAND

MAKING PAIN SACRED

As part of my own journey towards wholehearted confidence, I used meditation as a tool to explore my chronic pain, its greater meaning and my capacity to uncover new narratives relating to my experience.

There was one visualisation that created the most space for deep awareness and insight. It included creating the image of an altar, placing my pain on this altar, and then asking the pain, *What are you here to teach me? What would you have me know?*

During my own healing, I explored this practice many times. Sometimes the altar appeared as a large rock on a cliff's edge, other times it was a collection of shells on the beach. One time my imagination created an image of my pain as a collection of feathers, other times it presented as dark leathery kelp, or a perfectly shiny gold box. My imagination (and my deeper self) enjoyed this task!

Over the years I have guided thousands of people through a version of this meditation. Sometimes people are generous enough to share their experience.

Like Toby, who shared:

> *'The visualisation of the altar was a powerful and profound practice for me. I pictured myself hiking along a picturesque mountain trail at the peak of autumn. The air around me was crisp, cool and refreshingly clean. I relished the sights that surround me on the trail. I was in awe of the brilliant shades of marigold yellow, ruby red and fiery orange foliage on the vast trees along the trail. As I approached the peak of the mountain,*

the trailhead opened and expanded to expose a grassy meadow. In this meadow I saw the altar. It was a simple sacred space amidst the vastness of the mountain. I lovingly and tenderly placed my pain on that altar, an ultimate offering of release, honour and acceptance.'

People in my community have explored the pain of chronic illness, arthritis, cancer, divorce, infidelity, betrayal, job loss, car accidents, childhood trauma, mental health issues, loneliness and the death of parents and children. As I explained before, this meditation was only one of many tools they used to process their pain.

When they opened the lines of communication with their pain, here are some the messages they received:

- 'It's okay that you are a complicated person full of good and bad, celebrations and losses. You are safe to accept yourself.'
- 'Let the wound heal. You don't need to keep picking the scab.'
- 'You are safe to rest.'
- 'Take the time to pause and everything changes.'
- 'It's time to forgive yourself.'
- 'I am strong enough to be present with my physical pain. When I accept my pain, the sensation actually changes. It feels less overwhelming.'
- 'You are stronger than you realise.'
- 'There is always a part of me that is calm, even when other parts of me feel reactive.'
- 'It's time to let go.'
- 'Keep going, keep returning to yourself again and again with love, compassion and understanding. It is making a difference.'
- 'You are not your past.'

- 'Let people in.'
- 'There is no going back. Only moving forward, and that's okay.'
- 'The message was clear. It was always you. You are the love of your life.'

Are you feeling inspired or curious about placing your pain on an altar and receiving its message? If so, you can listen to this guided meditation on *The Happy Habit* app.

MAKING THE WORLD A WHOLEHEARTED PLACE

Throughout this book we have reflected upon how wholehearted confidence improves our own lives and our relationships. For example, when we acknowledge our own shadows, negativity bias and ego, we are more able to feel compassion towards others as they too meet with these conditioned beliefs and limitations. We have also explored how connecting with our hearts allows for less judgement, blame, separation and resentment towards others.

All these aspects of wholehearted confidence can be seen as implicit acts of service, as by strengthening our relationships and our sense of acceptance and understanding, we are indeed making a positive contribution to the world.

Even with this knowledge, many people in my meditation community expressed a belief that they were not making a meaningful difference.

Young people at the beginning of their careers felt like they didn't know enough about their unique skills and talents to be able to decide where to invest their giving energy. Older people in retirement felt unsure about ways they could use their time to contribute. Parents with young children, juggling multiple demands with work, family and domestic responsibilities felt too stretched to consider adding anything else to their list of responsibilities.

And so we cycle between a fear that we are not making a difference and a deep desire to contribute. How do we begin to bridge the divide? We start, as always, not with more actions or doing, but by pausing and expanding our awareness.

Do you remember when we explored equanimity, we practised holding our mistakes, regrets, challenges and life events in the vast sea of our awareness? We can do the same when examining being of service.

Start by reminding yourself that every small action you take creates a ripple. All those times you gently reminded your children to say please and thank you, to respect their elders and to be kind, has rippled out and created space for them to grow into respectful adults.

Acknowledge how, in the act of listening to a friend, you have helped to create a gentle wave of comfort and ease within the vast ocean of life.

Over time, you may even learn to expand your awareness far enough to not only see that your actions matter, but that you matter too - that you are part of the rhythm of life.

Every breath you take, every emotion you experience, every word you speak, creates energetic ripples. Each gesture of love or kindness, every laugh that bubbles up from deep within, every good intention flows out into life itself. This idea that who you are and how you feel radiates out into the world is supported by research. Let's explore the science together now.

RAISING YOUR VIBRATION & FEEDING THE FIELD

So firstly, what is a personal vibration, and do you have to wear yoga pants and be vegan to radiate a good vibe? The HeartMath Institute - a not-for-profit dedicated to providing solutions for activating the heart of humanity - defines it as the quality of the thoughts, feelings, attitudes and behaviours we experience throughout the day.

You don't need to identify as a spiritual person or wear a certain outfit in order to radiate a high vibration.

When people operate in a high vibration, they:

- act in alignment with their values.
- experience higher-quality emotions.
- are less self-absorbed and more balanced.
- are more able to creatively problem-solve.
- feel more self-secure.
- accumulate less stress.

When people operate in a lower vibration, they:

- act in ways that aren't in alignment with their values.
- experience lower-level emotions.
- are more self-absorbed and see everything in relation to themselves.

- get stuck in patterns of judgement, blame and resistance.
- ruminate and have trouble letting go of the past.
- accumulate stress in the body.

Perhaps you have a friend who always makes you feel good – it's not even the words spoken, it's more of a feeling. Somehow you always feel happy, satisfied and calm after seeing them. Chances are that this person is operating in a high vibration.

Conversely, maybe you know someone who just tends to bring you down and drain your energy? Or perhaps you've had the experience where someone says the right thing (like a meditation teacher, manager or friend) but for some reason, their words just don't ring true. Instead, they feel inauthentic or out of alignment. These people may be operating on a lower vibration.

So, how does their vibration affect you? Each heartbeat produces electricity, which in turn creates a magnetic field. This field radiates into the external environment about four feet in a 360-degree field. As Doc Childre, founder of the HeartMath Institute, explains:

> 'When our thoughts, emotions and attitudes are balanced and aligned, we radiate a measurably more coherent electromagnetic signal into the environment. This field can then be detected by the nervous systems of other people and animals. This explains why we can feel or sense another person's presence and emotional state, independent of body language or other factors.'

As a dog lover and wholehearted human, I love the research conducted by the HeartMath Institute and I hope you do too. The experiment used electrocardiogram monitors to record heart-rhythm data on Josh, a fifteen-year-old boy, and his dog Mabel - when they were together and apart.

The heart monitors revealed that, when Josh entered the room where Mabel was waiting and consciously felt feelings of love and care towards his dog, his heart rhythms became more coherent.

Consequently, Mabel's heart rhythms also became more coherent. The experiment also concluded that when Mabel received Josh's heart coherence, she became more affectionate, animated and connected. When Josh left the room, Mabel's heart rhythms became much more chaotic and incoherent, suggesting initial separation anxiety.

The point of sharing this research is not to make you feel guilty for leaving your dog at home alone when you go to work! It is to illustrate how powerful taking the time to cultivate a sense of gladness, appreciation, love and connection in your heart is for those around you.

As their electromagnetic field becomes more coherent, they become more able to cultivate and express affection, emotion and feelings of connection too. This in turn allows them to share their heart coherence with others. And so, the coherent electromagnetic ripple continues.

MAKE A POSITIVE CONTRIBUTION TO OUR SHARED VIBRATIONAL FIELD IN THREE EASY STEPS

Step one:

For one week, take time each day to raise your own vibration. Here are five ideas to get you started:

1. Do one thing that is in alignment with your values.
2. Practise gratitude.
3. Move on, forgive yourself or someone else.
4. Try and see something from someone else's perspective.
5. Do something to reduce stress like meditation, yoga or walking in nature.

Step two:

Every day for one week, do the visualisation Strengthening Your Field explained on the following page and enhance your capacity to create a coherent field.

Step three:

Practise, practise, practise. Become an expert at connecting with your heart and sensing into the field you radiate outwards. Take a few minutes before you go to the shops, drive your car, take your dog for a walk, pick your kids up from school, see your parents - to feed the common field. Be curious and playful.

Notice if your vibration and your commitment to making a positive contribution to the field makes a difference. Do your kids feel more calm? Is there less fighting between the siblings? Did someone smile at you in the supermarket? Were your parents more affectionate and caring towards you? Enjoy the possibility that you are creating positive energetic ripples. Allow these small but significant moments to land by feeling them in your body, and of course, in your heart!

EXPAND

VISUALISATION PRACTICE STRENGTHENING YOUR FIELD

Take a moment in the wholehearted posture. Sky. Body. Earth.
For a few breaths, focus on your chest and then your heart.

As you breathe in repeat: *I invite a sense of openness, gratitude and compassion into my heart.*

As you breathe out, repeat: *I let go of judgement, blame and fear.*
Trust that, as you do this, you are creating a sense of inner balance and harmony.

Imagine the coherent electromagnetic field that radiates from your heart four feet into the environment. Get creative as you imagine it having a colour and a texture.

Now imagine that someone you love or like enters your field (perhaps a pet, family member or close friend).

Create the image in your mind's eye that they are basking in your electromagnetic field. Notice their body, mind and heart receiving this positive vibration that you are radiating.

Now, imagine yourself moving through your day, going to work, the shops, interacting with family and friends. Picture every person or animal you get close to benefiting from your balanced and compassionate electromagnetic field.

Repeat silently in your mind: *I contribute to the world by feeding the vibrational field. Strengthening the field is an act of service.*

CONFIDENCE IN ACTION - COHERENCE IN THE CLASSROOM

Alex is a primary school teacher who lives in Australia. His job was especially challenging during the pandemic when staff, parents and students were all feeling the effects of lockdowns, restrictions and uncertainty.

Alex has spent much of his adult life thinking he always needs a big goal or project to be working towards. Whilst the possibility of a large project or aspiration to work towards is inspiring, it also creates a certain level of stress or distraction for him.

During the wholehearted confidence process, Alex discovered that living his values every day and bringing a sense of presence and flow to anything that comes his way (both the joys and the challenges), may actually be a more rewarding way to live.

As part of his commitment to trying new things and cultivating more presence and flow, Alex began to take his dog, Pepper, into the classroom. He realised pretty quickly that Pepper was an amazing tool who was able to relax upset or triggered kids almost instantly.

Alex reflected on how much he enjoyed having Pepper in the classroom and how much more calm and present he felt with his students when his furry friend was by his side. Alex enjoyed meeting the version of himself who surfaced when Pepper was there. He was fun, kind and relaxed, very different to the burnt-out and stressed Alex of before.

When I imagine Alex, Pepper and all the children in this classroom, I picture a whole lot of coherent hearts and electromagnetic fields all connecting with each other! If only they each had an electrocardiogram monitor, we could have contributed to the HeartMath research!

Alex's experience is a powerful reminder that we can be of service through our commitment to presence, flow, creativity and fun. When we tap into our light and playful nature, it feels easier and more natural to be a force of good in the world.

PART FOUR: SELF-REFLECTION

Wholehearted confidence is about opening the lines of communication with your body, heart and the natural world. By learning to access intelligence from a source greater than your mind, it feels easier to live your values, be authentic and make both wise and courageous decisions. By accessing this great pool of intelligence, you can unhook from the drama and the stories that keep you small. You can respond to your challenges and relationships with greater perspective and compassion.

But let's remind ourselves one final time that learning to trust life, and our place within it, isn't about spiritual bypassing. It doesn't include responding to our own pain or the pain of another with throwaway phrases like 'everything happens for a reason' or 'the universe has a message for you'.

We still traverse the ups and downs of our emotional landscape. We continue to engage in moments of vulnerability. But we do so in ways that allow us to feel less reactive and pulled in, and more open and grounded. As one community member reflected, 'I am learning to hold it all, my own suffering, the tragedies of the world, all the incredible miracles of my life and the beautiful world we inhabit with wholehearted confidence.'

Take a moment to answer these four questions:

1. In my life right now, would opening the lines of communication with my body, heart or the natural world make me feel most wholeheartedly confident?
2. Which of my relationships could benefit from me cultivating greater equanimity?
3. Who do I feel most excited about sharing my heart coherence with?
4. What has been the biggest revelation for me throughout this book?

A TRANSCENDENT EXPERIENCE

By now, I hope you have discovered that wholehearted confidence is so much more than being able to stroll into a party feeling totally self-assured, public speak without nerves or feel assured of your next move.

I also hope that you know it's an ongoing journey, not a 'one and done' experience. Trust that, if you continue along the wholehearted confidence path, there will be moments of great insight, healing and humour. You may even be greeted with a transcendent experience.

You might remember Rose, the woman from part one who, as a young girl, loved to paint but was ridiculed by her elder brother? Throughout the wholehearted confidence process, Rose was open, curious and enthusiastic. Consequently, she had many revelations.

She finally understood the significance of events from her past and how they impacted her adult self. She befriended her shadow of procrastination, forgave family members, lived more from her values and explored the positive flow-on effects of embodying the wholehearted posture when out and about.

But the most transcendent experience occurred when Rose listened to the guided meditation on exploring pain. During the practice, Rose was transported back in time to May 1991 - the day her eleven-year-old daughter was killed in an accident while playing with a friend.

The memory of the pain was so visceral. Rose felt a physical jolt, like an electrical shock move through her body.

During the meditation, Rose imagined the altar as a large boulder in the mountains near where she lives in America. In her mind's eye, it was sunset. The pain showed up as a black, almost tear-shaped velvet bag. When she opened it, a black mist or cloud emerged from the bag.

'It wasn't threatening or scary. It felt like it wanted to be freed,' explained Rose. She took a moment to befriend it. She thanked it for showing up and then she asked the questions:

What are you here to teach me? What would you have me know?

It responded by saying in a very calm, compassionate way that it was here to teach Rose to let go; to release the past and those things she had no control over. It gently reminded her that holding onto the pain wouldn't alter the outcome. The pain wanted Rose to know that Brigid's leaving was her choice, she chose not to come back because she would never be the person she had been before.

EXPAND

Rose thanked the pain again for showing up and for communicating with her. Buoyed by her commitment to wholehearted confidence, she was able to release the pain.

'Until that moment, I wasn't aware of how exhausting it has been carrying around the pain,' she said, 'I have to say, while it was a bit wrenching to go through the replay of that event so graphically, I feel like a boulder has been lifted off me! By holding onto the pain, I've been holding myself captive to an event that happened more than thirty years ago. I have thought about this one event probably tens of thousands of times and never experienced it the way I did during this guided meditation.'

At the end of the meditation, Rose set herself an intention. *When I think of my beautiful girl, Brigid, I will live in the light of her life, not the moment of her death.*

A few days after this meditation experience, the spirit of young Brigid came to visit Rose. She had a message for her mother.

She was elated that her mum had released the pain, and in doing so, she was able to release her sadness and sense of responsibility at the devastation her death caused. Brigid told Rose that, sometimes, she couldn't see her mother, only the boulder of pain. Rose knew that carrying around the pain impacted her daughter's peace on the other side.

As a mother, she was happy to still be able to help her child find peace and happiness. Rose commented, 'She is still my child, we just meet and talk in different ways now.'

I kept in touch with Rose over the months following this deep experience of letting go and healing. In one email Rose wrote, 'This experience has truly been transcendent. There is no hint of the pain returning, my mind, my body, my emotional self and my spirit feel free. I truly feel like a huge boulder was lifted off me that day in meditation.'

For the first time in thirty years, Rose was able to celebrate her daughter's birthday without the lens of pain directing the focus.

Rose and Brigid's story reminds us that it's never too late to heal, to expand our belief systems and our capacity to connect to a source of intelligence that lives beyond our mind and our immediate environment. It is an invitation to remember that love is a universal energy that can travel time and space.

It feels incredibly poetic to have opened this book with Rose's story - a childhood recollection from over sixty years ago - and now to close with her transcendent experience of healing. It shows what is possible when you are committed to embracing change, no matter your age or the personal tragedy you have experienced.

I hope this story has inspired and comforted you, as it certainly has for me.

EXPAND

YOUR
CONFIDENCE
COMMITMENTS

Repeat these phrases in the morning or at night either out loud or in your mind. Write them in your journal or on a Post-it Note. Use them anytime you want to drop into the feeling of wholehearted confidence.

I listen to and respect my body.

I take time each day to pause and connect to the wisdom in my heart.

I allow emotions to move through my body without getting hooked into the stories.

I create opportunities for nature to be my teacher.

I notice when I am feeling overwhelmed by my care for others, and I practise equanimity.

I trust that when my heart is coherent, I can make a difference in the world.

EPILOGUE

The Mapmaker and the Traveller

You might remember that I began this book with a reflection on how I trusted my own voice and didn't need the external validation of my editor? It's worth noting that this inner trust didn't excuse me from the inevitable moments of self-doubt and vulnerability that naturally surface when writing a book.

It did, however, allow me to surrender to the process and not feel pulled in by these more tender moments. Wholehearted confidence invited me to embrace the possibility of being both teacher and student, or, in the words of Brené Brown, both mapmaker and traveller.

After teaching the wholehearted confidence framework to thousands of people around the world, witnessing people's transformations, documenting their stories and collating all the feedback into themes, I began to write.

Within a week, I experienced a chronic pain flare-up. Familiar pain in my back, shoulders, neck, wrists and hands. New pain in my knees and hips. A tug of war between my desire to express myself and my fear of being judged was playing out. My body was the stage.

In the past, I may have believed the stories swirling around in my mind. Inner narratives fuelled by my ego like, *Every time you try and do something important or meaningful your chronic pain gets worse, you should just stop trying.*

This time around, I filled my life with opportunities to feel safe and nurtured. Morning meditation, early nights, lots of walks with my dog. Through these actions I sent a message to my body that it was safe, and that together, we were going to write this book, even if it felt uncomfortable.

As I wrote about exploring our shadows, my own came to visit. Imposter syndrome and high expectations joined forces in an attempt to take me off course. Whilst committing to making my framework more inclusive, these shadows whispered, *Who are you to talk about trauma?* and, *You need to get this discussion exactly right so as not to offend, exclude or silence anyone's experience or voice.*

I danced with these shadows. I felt their expression within my body. Heavy. Dull. Constricting. With the aid of my breath and wholehearted awareness, I moved beyond these conditioned responses to the wisdom that resided below. I received the message, *This book is important to you. Your desire is for all those who read it to feel seen and heard.* I allowed these words to be my North Star, to soften my shadows.

When I was deep in part three, I noticed that, like George, I too was in the habit of deflecting compliments and feeling the need to reciprocate feelings of gratitude or praise.

Someone surprised me with a bunch of flowers and my immediate thought was, *I will gift them a copy of my book.* When I noticed this knee-jerk response to feeling valued by others I took a deep breath, placed my hand on my heart and felt into the appreciation. Thank you, George!

And of course, as I wrote part four, nature appeared in high definition. I experienced an awakened sensitivity to the vitality of the morning birds, the feel of the cool breeze on my skin, the dappled light across the grass

HOLD YOUR CHILDHOOD WITH TENDER HANDS.

LIVE FROM YOUR VALUES.

DANCE WITH YOUR SHADOWS.

REMEMBER YOUR INHERENT GOODNESS.

at dusk. As I invited the readers to hold their lives in the vast ocean of awareness, I too became more aware of my place in the natural ebb and flow of life.

In truth, some of this clarity felt uncomfortable, especially the part where I saw with a fresh perspective just how privileged I am. I observed myself living in a country where I am safe to express my opinions and speak from the heart whilst so many others around the world are not. I recognised the privilege of having enough financial security to write a book, whilst others live in poverty or under financial strain.

I felt into the gift of having access to education and training that helps me move beyond my egoic mind towards a fuller experience of life. Whilst I will never understand all the layers of my privilege, I am committed to uncovering these and keeping them in mind and heart as I engage with my personal and professional communities and walk the wholehearted confidence path.

Sometimes, in the spiritual world, phrases like 'we are all one' are thrown about. Whilst this may be true from a biological or energetic perspective, it's been drawn to my attention recently how dismissive these comments can be for individuals and communities who have been born into poverty, subject to systemic racism, prejudice or persecution, or live with chronic physical, emotional or mental conditions.

Wholehearted confidence must therefore include a willingness to engage in conversations and activities that create space for people from all corners of the globe to feel seen, heard and empowered to break free from cycles of poverty and systemic disadvantage.

Whilst our expression of wholehearted confidence is dynamic and will change over time, as I write this epilogue, an important component of my journey is using my skills as a meditation teacher to contribute to positive social and environmental change.

My business, *The Happy Habit*, operates as a social enterprise that redistributes 50% of profits to support grassroots projects tackling poverty. My commitment is to provide 80,000 people with a permanent source of drinking water by 2025. By purchasing this book, you have allowed your own desire for inner confidence to contribute to the lives of others. Thank you.

Perhaps, after reading this book, you feel inspired to donate or volunteer your time, share your expertise with greater intention, sign more petitions or communicate with your local government? Maybe you feel drawn to speaking less and listening more, to prioritising understanding over judgement? Or are you keen to teach your children or grandchildren how to meditate or feed the communal field with their heart coherence?

Trust in your unique ability to radiate wholehearted confidence. Try this final practice and discover where, and how, you feel drawn to making a difference.

MINDFUL PRACTICE
WHOLEHEARTED HANDS

For one final time, enjoy the wholehearted posture. Imagine the sky smiling down upon you. Feel this smile in your heart. Radiate this gesture of warmth and receptivity into the earth beneath you.

Take a few deep breaths into your heart. Activate feelings of gladness, gratitude and presence.

As you connect with your heart, remind yourself of our shared humanity. Remember that every human deserves to be seen, heard and recognised for who they are. Every human is entitled to live a life of hope, freedom and fairness.

Imagine that the energy you have just generated in your heart has a colour, a texture or a pulse. Really feel it in your heart.

Picture this energy travelling like a river across the width of your shoulders, down your arms, into your hands and fingers.

Notice any sensation (warmth, tingling, aliveness) in your hands. Really connect with the energy within your hands. You may even like to rub your hands together as a way to increase the sensation.

Ask yourself: *How will I use these hands of mine to make a positive contribution to the world?*

Listen. Receive. Trust.

Remember that no act is too small.

Take wholehearted action from this place of wisdom and insight.

As we come to the end of this book, we are reminded that wholehearted confidence provides a framework to live, love and contribute. Take a moment to reflect on these three questions:

1. What would *living* each day with wholehearted confidence look and feel like for you?
2. How could you use wholehearted confidence to strengthen the *love* you have for yourself and others?
3. How do you feel most inspired to *contribute?*

Through wholehearted confidence, we can liberate ourselves from the pervasive cultures of scarcity, grind and separation. Hold your childhood with tender hands. Live from your values. Dance with your shadows. Remember your inherent goodness. Allow the wisdom from your body, heart and natural world to guide you. Dare to hold the joys and the sorrows in the vast sea of your awareness.

Take this wholehearted confidence framework and magnify it with your unique expression. And never forget to have fun along the way!

ACKNOWLEDGEMENTS

Thank you to my boys, Andrew, Tom, Gabe and Dash, for filling our home, and my life, with love, laughter, long hugs, random dance moves and toilet humour.

Thank you to my international meditation community, especially those committed, generous, honest and trusting students who participated in my various research groups and courses. Your stories breathed life and colour into my wholehearted confidence framework, making it more rich, real and inspiring.

Thank you to all the spiritual teachers, neuroscientists, psychotherapists and psychologists who have committed their lives to sharing their knowledge and wisdom. Your research, perspectives and frameworks have helped me on my personal and professional path.

To Eliza Todd, the incredibly talented illustrator of this book. Thanks for saying 'yes' to a stranger from the other side of the world. In gratitude to you for your gentle heart, kind nature and genuine desire to create art that helps people accept their vulnerabilities, embrace who they are and put one foot in front of the other when life feels hard.

To Amy Molloy, my editor and friend. Beyond generous and capable, you make editing books look easy! Writing a book is a creative, and at times, lonely process. Knowing you were there, by my side, ready to hear about the weird and wonderful synchronicities and the evolution of my writer's journey was a gift.

To Karen McDermott, my publisher, for giving me total freedom and autonomy. Your positive and light-filled approach makes the whole process feel intuitive, free-flowing and exciting. Thank you for trusting in my vision and for supporting me to create more beautiful things next year.

To Bree Hankinson, the designer of this book. I love working and laughing with you. Thanks for being so laid back, creative, understated, clever and fun to work with. I am excited to see what we create next!

Thank you to all my female friends, many of whom I have met much later in life. Gratitude to you, Nancy, Tesh, Freya, Lisa, Jus, Amy, Kate, Jo and Christey. Our walks, swims, stand-up paddleboards and coffees fill my cup. Our conversations about spirituality, work-life balance, creativity, philanthropy, food, meditation, midlife, teenagers, courage and pain all help me show up, write and live with greater clarity and truth.

Finally, thank you to everyone who has read this book, passed it onto their friends and family, and helped to spread the message. You are part of a ripple effect which will change our global attitude to confidence and what it feels like to be comfortable and at home in both our internal and external worlds. Thank you for being part of the journey.

REFERENCES

Part 1

Levine, P. 2005, *Trauma and Memory*

Mate, G. 2022, *The Myth of Normal*

Maslow, A. 1964, *Religions, Values and Peak Experiences*

Maslow, A. 1991, *Towards a psychology of being*

Privette, G. 2001, 'Defining moments of self-actualization: Peak performance and peak experience', T*he Handbook of Humanistic Psychology*, pp. 161-180

Privette, G. 1983, 'Peak experience, peak performance, and flow: A comparative analysis of positive human experiences', *Journal of Personality and Social Psychology*, Vol. 45, No. 6

Salzberg, S. 2020, *Loving Kindness, The Revolutionary Art of Happiness*

Ekman, P. 2004, *Emotions Revealed*

Matsumoto, D. and Willingham, B. 2009, 'Spontaneous Facial Expressions of Emotion in Congenitally and Non-Congenitally Blind Individuals', *The Journal of Personality and Social Psychology,* Vol. 96, No.1

Lieberman, M. 2013, *Social: Why our brains are wired to connect*

Part Two

Schwartz, R. 2021, *No Bad Parts*

Brach, T. 2001, 'Awakening from the trance of unworthiness', *Inquiring Mind*, Vol. 17, No 2

Brown, B. 2012, *Daring Greatly*

Clance, P. and Imes, S. 1978, 'The Impostor Phenomenon in High Achieving Women: Dynamics and Therapeutic Interventions'. *Psychology and Psychotherapy: Theory, Research and Practice*, Vol. 15, pp. 241-247

Young, V. 2011, *The secret thoughts of successful women*

Langford, J. and Clance, P. 1993, 'The impostor phenomenon: recent research findings regarding dynamics, personality and family patterns and their implications for treatment, *Psychotherapy: Theory, Research, Practice, Training*. Vol. 30, No. 3

Brummelman, E., Thomaes, S., Overbeek, G., Orobio de Castro, B., Van den Hout, M. and Bushman, B. 2014, 'On feeding those hungry for praise: Person praise backfires in children with low self-esteem', *Journal of Experimental Psychology: General*, Vol. 143, No. 1

Winnicott, D. 2005, *Playing and Reality*

Van der Kolk, B. 2015, *The Body Keeps the Score*

Part 3

Dr Hanson, R and Hanson, F. 2018, *Resilient: How to Grow an Unshakable Core of Calm, Strength, and Happiness*

Chodron, P. 1997, *When Things Fall Apart*

Salzberg, S. 2013, *Real Happiness at Work: Meditations for Accomplishment, Achievement and Peace*

Part 4

Salzberg, S. 2020, *Real Change: Mindfulness to Heal Ourselves and the World*

Van Der Kolk, V. 2015, *The Body Keeps the Score*

Bradshaw, J. 1988, *Healing the Shame that Binds You*

Plutchik, R. 1991, *The Emotions*

Tolle, E. 2006, *The Power of Now*

Bolte-Taylor, J. 2009, *My Stroke of Insight*

Childre, D. and Martin, H. 2000, *The Heartmath Solution: The Institute of Heartmath's Revolutionary Program for Engaging the Power of the Heart's Intelligence*

Childre, D., Rozman, D. and McCraty, R. 2022, *Heart Intelligence: Connecting with the Heart's Intuitive Guidance for Effective Choices and Solutions*

Allen, S. 2018, 'The Science of Awe', Prepared by The Greater Good Science Center at CU Berkeley

Welwood, J. 2002, *Toward a Psychology of Awakening*

ABOUT THE AUTHOR

Fleur Chambers is a multi-award-winning meditation teacher, creator of *The Happy Habit* app, bestselling author and philanthropist. Through her guided meditations, courses and books, Fleur is helping people all around the world say yes to their entire lives, even the challenges and setbacks.

With proceeds from *The Happy Habit* funding grassroots projects in some of the poorest communities around the world, Fleur is using meditation as a tool for social change. By 2025 The Happy Habit will have provided 80,000 people with a permanent source of drinking water.

Often referred to by her students as gentle, curious and warm-hearted, Fleur reminds us that there is strength in softness and that we are safe to be ourselves.

ABOUT THE ILLUSTRATOR

Eliza Todd is the artist and illustrator behind the brand A Peace of Werk. She is a mixed media artist who licenses her art to brands for stationery and home decor worldwide.

Through her brand A Peace of Werk, Eliza strives to create art that is uplifting and encourages us to remember that through all of life's ups and downs there is beauty and richness to be found in the journey.

You can follow her on her Instagram page @apeaceofwerk or visit her at www.apeaceofwerk.com

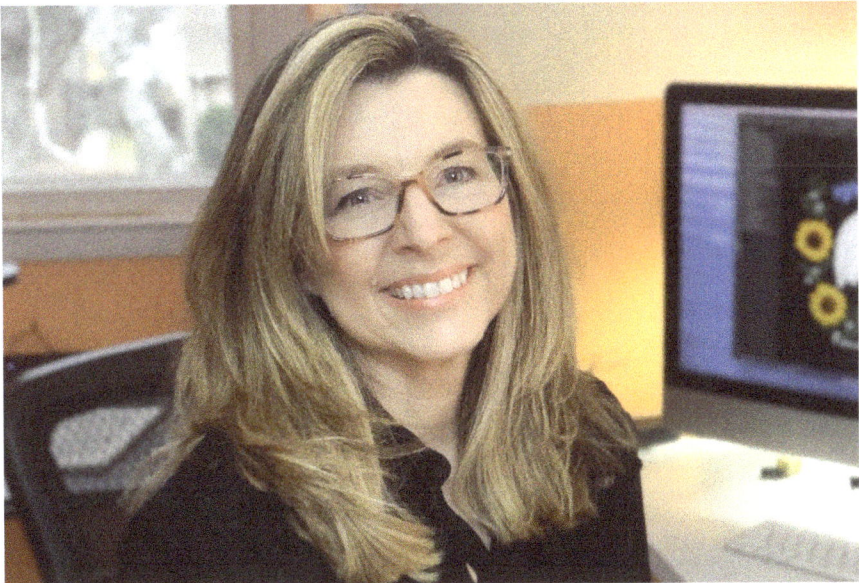

Milton Keynes UK
Ingram Content Group UK Ltd.
UKHW051054290124
436883UK00008B/125

9 780645 867046